UNCONVENTIONAL DIPLOMACY IN SOUTHERN AFRICA

Unconventional Diplomacy in Southern Africa

Robin Renwick

St. Martin's Press
New York

St. Martin's Press, Scholarly and Reference Division,
175 Fifth Avenue, New York, N.Y. 10010

First published in the United States of America in 1997

This book is printed on paper suitable for recycling and
made from fully managed and sustained forest sources.

Printed in Great Britain

ISBN 0–312–16533–1

Library of Congress Cataloging-in-Publication Data
Renwick, Robin.
Unconventional diplomacy in Southern Africa / Robin Renwick.
p.   cm.
Includes bibliographical references and index.
ISBN 0–312–16533–1
1. Zimbabwe—History—Chimurenga War, 1966–1980—Peace.
2. Zimbabwe—Foreign relations—Great Britain.   3. Great Britain–
–Foreign relations—Zimbabwe.   4. Namibia—Politics and
government—1946–1990.   5. Insurgency—Namibia—History—20th
century.   6. Namibia—Foreign relations—Great Britain.   7. Great
Britain—Foreign relations—Namibia.   8. Renwick, Robin.   I. Title.
DT2994.R46   1997
968.91'04—dc20   96–32086
                                                                      CIP

Contents

Preface

At Lancaster House I was involved in the last of many attempts to resolve the Rhodesia problem. This is an account of that experience. It is dedicated to Christopher Soames who, shortly before he died, told me that he had not had the chance to write about his adventures in Rhodesia and hoped that I would do so instead.

Having served as British Ambassador to South Africa at the time, I have sought also to give an account of the Namibia settlement and of events in the period immediately preceding and following the release of Nelson Mandela.

Part I
The Rhodesia Settlement

1 A Long-standing Source of Grief

In November 1978 I was appointed head of the Rhodesian Department in the Foreign and Commonwealth Office. It was not a post for which there were many other candidates at the time. Rhodesia posed in an acute form the problem of responsibility without power. Britain, nominally at least, had the constitutional responsibility for the territory and constantly was reminded of it by the rest of the Commonwealth, who used this as a stick with which to beat successive British governments – Labour and Conservative. But the army and police were controlled by the Rhodesians and had been since the Colony was granted what amounted to dominion status in 1923.

The intrinsic difficulties had been compounded by the way the problem was tackled. As Ian Smith prepared unilaterally to declare Rhodesia's independence in November 1965, Harold Wilson ruled out publicly the use of force to deal with such an act of defiance. No British government was prepared to use force in Rhodesia, but the wisdom of announcing this in advance has been questioned ever since. This was followed by Wilson's statement at the Commonwealth Conference in Lagos in January 1966 that sanctions might bring the rebellion to an end 'within a matter of weeks rather than months'. Working in the African Department of the Foreign Office at the time, I was at a loss to know why the Prime Minister had said this. It turned out to have been on the advice of an official from the newly created – and soon to be abolished – Department of Economic Affairs. Harold Wilson never lived the statement down.

Following the failure of Wilson's negotiations with Ian Smith, the Conservatives returned to power determined to try to reach an agreement with him. Alec Douglas-Home managed to do so, largely through the good offices of Lord Goodman, and on the basis of granting independence with Smith still in charge, in return for a constitution which was supposed to lead eventually to majority rule. Alec Douglas-Home was a most honourable man. He believed sincerely that the alternative was worse. But this 'solution' depended on Ian Smith acting as honourably as Sir Alec would have done, which I doubted, fearing that Smith would take independence and then block any further African advance – finally destroying Britain's reputation. We were rescued from this dilemma by the African population, led by Bishop Muzorewa, who made clear that they had no faith whatever that Ian Smith and his colleagues would carry out their promises.

Since then, things had gone from bad to worse and the Department was at the nadir of its fortunes. The problem had become, as Margaret Thatcher was to put it, 'a long-standing source of grief to successive British governments'. The Anglo-American proposals worked out by David Owen and the US Secretary of State, Cyrus Vance, had been rejected both by the Rhodesians and by Joshua Nkomo and Robert Mugabe, who had formed an alliance known as the Patriotic Front. The war was getting worse and the Labour government had little domestic support for its policy.

My first task was to attend the parliamentary debates on the Bingham Report, which concluded that the British oil companies had connived at the evasion of oil sanctions against Rhodesia, with the acquiescence of the Wilson government. Harold Wilson claimed to have known nothing about the matter, despite his office having been told about it by his Minister, George Thomson. George Thomson made a dignified statement, saying that he had indeed known about the oil 'swaps', but since the Labour government was not prepared to try to apply oil sanctions to the whole of southern Africa, there was no way in which supplies could be prevented from reaching Rhodesia. The debates made painful listening.

They were followed by the resignation of Field-Marshal Carver, whom David Owen had hoped to instal as British Resident Commissioner in Rhodesia to oversee elections and independence. Carver resigned because he saw no chance of Ian Smith, Nkomo or Mugabe agreeing. Instead he expected a steady intensification of the guerrilla war, leading eventually to a near-complete breakdown of law and order in which many of the whites would have to be evacuated.

This certainly seemed to be the safest prophecy at the time. But Owen still hankered after a conference at which he hoped some progress might be made. Cledwyn Hughes, a respected former Labour Minister, was sent off on yet another fruitless pilgrimage around southern Africa. On his return, he reported that a conference would have no chance of success. Ian Smith was determined to proceed with a settlement with the internal parties, led by Muzorewa. Nkomo and Mugabe believed they could obtain their objectives through an intensification of the war. Neither side was prepared to participate in elections in circumstances which would give the other any chance of winning.

As Ian Smith, on the basis of his agreement with Muzorewa, declared his intention of holding elections in which, for the first time, the entire Rhodesian population would be able to vote, David Owen set off for Washington for consultations with Vance. The Carter Administration was struggling and it was not hard to see why. Cyrus Vance impressed as a decent and honourable, but not very forceful, Secretary of State, generally worsted in internecine battles by the National Security Advisor, Zbigniew Brzezinski. When Vance's officials, led by Tony Lake, subsequently National Security Advisor under President Clinton, extolled the virtues of the Anglo-American proposals, Owen pointed out that, unfortunately, the only people who agreed with them were the British and Americans. But they did have the advantage, from the Carter Administration's point of view, of appealing to the other African governments and to the black caucus in Congress, as a way of ensuring non-recognition of a future Muzorewa regime.

It was agreed that a joint effort should be made to convince the South Africans that they should dissuade Smith from proceeding with the internal settlement. This looked a pretty forlorn hope as the South African objective was to see a 'moderate' black government take over in Rhodesia. Preparing instructions to our Ambassadors in the field proved something of a nightmare, as the Foreign Office practice was to tell the Embassy the objective to be aimed for, leaving it to decide how best to deploy the relevant arguments. The State Department practice was to give their Ambassadors detailed speaking notes to be used verbatim and left behind afterwards. As it took me several days to negotiate the text of a single telegram with my State Department colleagues, a certain amount of iron began to enter into my soul about this way of operating.

The South Africans rejected this *démarche*. The Labour government was sruggling through the 'winter of discontent'. David Owen's relations with the Foreign Office hierarchy were fraught as a result of what they considered to be his desire to try to do everything himself and his conviction that the normal procedures frequently were interminably laborious.

My own relations with David Owen were good and in March 1979 I suddenly was instructed by him and Vance to go to Rhodesia with an American colleague, Stephen Low, the US Ambassador in Lusaka, to report on the situation and the chances of persuading Smith and his colleagues not to proceed with the April elections and instead to enter all-party negotiations.

Personally, I thought the chances of that were nil. But I welcomed the chance to get to Rhodesia and meet the principal actors in this drama. The method of getting there, as it turned out, was to provide some drama of its own.

From Johannesburg I was offered a lift by Low on the aircraft of the US Military Attaché in Pretoria. Nkomo's ZIPRA guerrillas recently had shot down two civilian aircraft of Air Rhodesia with SAM missiles. As we arrived over Salisbury, the aircraft had to descend in a sharp twisting spiral, in an effort to avoid another ZIPRA exploit with their SAMs.

Despite the increasingly desperate situation in the rural areas, Salisbury still appeared strangely unaffected by the war. The African townships showed better housing and greater prosperity than in most other parts of the continent. Conditions were very different on the outskirts of the city, where ramshackle camps housed the thousands of refugees from the rural areas seeking escape from the fighting. Within the European city, streets lined with flowering trees gave an impression of calm and orderliness. But travel outside the city after mid-afternoon was strongly advised against.

I had last seen Bishop Muzorewa when he was leading the opposition to the Smith–Home proposals. As the only internal African leader with any real political support – and he did have quite a lot at the time – he was confident of winning the election and becoming Prime Minister. He believed that once a black Prime Minister was installed, many of the guerrillas would lay down their arms. He intended to offer them an amnesty. Ian Smith already was indicating that he would want to participate in the new government. Muzorewa had been told that this would be necessary to maintain white confidence. Displaying an extraordinary political naiveté, he seemed oblivious to the extent to which Smith's continued presence would reduce the chances of international recognition and lose the regime African support. His rival Sithole still was expressing confidence, which no one else shared, that he would win more seats than Muzorewa, whom he regarded as inept.

The most important of our meetings was with the Commander of Joint Operations, General Peter Walls. Among the Rhodesian commanders, he was the dominant personality. Rhodesian-born, he had served with distinction with the Black Watch in Malaysia. Accustomed to leading his men from the front – himself frequently accompanying them on operations – Walls at the time was hero-worshipped by most white Rhodesians and seen by them as the real successor to Ian Smith.

Walls had no doubt of his ability to hold the guerrillas at bay while elections were held. Mugabe's ZANLA guerrillas had apparently inexhaustible reserves of manpower. But they were poorly equipped and were being pushed across the border as soon as they were trained. Nkomo's men had more heavy equipment than they could use, but no air cover.

Walls was conscious that Nkomo so far had committed only a fraction of his forces inside Rhodesia. To counter both threats the Rhodesians were relying more and more on cross-border operations, disrupting infiltration plans and forcing a further dispersal of the guerrilla camps. The Rhodesians were busy arming groups in the western provinces of Mozambique opposed to the government in Maputo – thereby helping to create what was to become RENAMO. There was no effective military co-ordination between ZIPRA and Mugabe's ZANLA, and there were periodic clashes between them. Walls ('I am not a Smith man') could see no alternative to proceeding with the internal settlement. He did not see how plans for internationally supervised elections would work. A UN force would not be able to cope with the forces already on the ground inside Rhodesia. If the security forces were confined to barracks, the guerrillas would take over the local population.

Ian Smith had absented himself during this visit. His deputy and Finance Minister, David Smith, acknowledged the horrendous economic problems being posed by the war and that the limits of white manpower had very nearly been reached. The representatives of other sections of opinion painted a gloomy picture of the situation across the country. In Bulawayo there was a universal conviction that Matabeleland was solidly for Nkomo. Members of the African Farmers' Union gave a graphic description of the fate of the rural population, harassed in turn by the army, auxiliaries and guerrillas, the latter arriving during the night to kill or punish those who had collaborated during the day. The Red Cross were concerned about the deliberate withholding of food supplies by the army from guerrilla-affected areas. The Catholic Justice and Peace Commission showed an equal concern about the fate of the rural population, for whom the main requirement was an end to the war.

There followed a dinner at Meikles Hotel given by the remarkable head of the Rhodesian Central Intelligence Organization, Ken Flower. He was accompanied by his deputy, Derrick Robinson, who on behalf of the regime had conducted innumerable negotiations with Nkomo, for whose return he showed an evident nostalgia. Flower was unconvinced. He believed that Nkomo's support by now was reduced to the Ndebele and they represented less than one-fifth of the population. If Nkomo committed his conventional battalions, based in Zambia, to an attack across the Zambesi in an effort to disrupt the elections, they would be decimated. I pressed him on the extent of Mugabe's support. That, Flower acknowledged, was a different matter. Mugabe conceivably could win an election. But he was far too extreme for any attempt at a negotiation with him to be worth making.

None of the rural areas was now secure. ZIPRA and ZANLA controlled large areas of the countryside. Severe pressure was being exerted on the farming community and travel was not safe anywhere in Rhodesia. There were sporadic incidents on the outskirts of Salisbury and a curfew was in operation within a few miles of the city centre. But half the white population lived in the capital in areas unaffected by the war. No one believed that the Patriotic Front could win an early military victory. The crucial factor in deciding whether the military balance tipped in favour of the Front was going to be white morale. They were already carrying a disproportionately heavy burden of military service.

Many of the whites made clear that they would be waiting to see if the April elections produced any improvement in the security situation or some prospect of the lifting of sanctions. If they did, they would stay on. If not, there would be a further exodus. This would take some time to affect the security forces. But it would depress the economy and progressively deprive the army of the reinforcement provided by the call-up of white reservists, all of whom were being mobilized for the elections.

The turnout in the elections looked likely to be significant not so much as an indication of the true support of the internal leaders, but rather as a demonstration of the extent to which the regime or the Front were in effective control of the population. The regime was trying belatedly to operate a form of constitutional advance – in which the whites would retain most of the levers of control – with the only one of the three African parties (that of Muzorewa) which had real popular support. The whites had made those concessions under the pressure of the war. But those who had been applying that pressure were excluded.

At the airport, *en route* to Mozambique via Johannesburg, I encountered a group of young Rhodesians in wheelchairs, all of them victims of land-mines. In Maputo, Mugabe operated from a broken-down block of flats on the outskirts of the city. In a scene the exact counterpart of the one I had witnessed at Salisbury airport, outside his office were congregated a group of young black Zimbabweans, all of them mutilated by war injuries. The difference was that they did not have wheelchairs. The city of Maputo had reached a state of dilapidation which seemed designed to make the Rhodesians' point about what would happen if the whites left and 'standards' no longer were maintained. Nor were things any better elsewhere in Mozambique. President Machel himself had just declared that in the port of Beira the weeds had grown so high, he could have concealed another liberation army there!

Robert Mugabe received me surrounded by his Central Committee. For ZANU's was a collective leadership. Reserved, almost shy in manner, Mugabe at first impression seemed more cut out for the priesthood than for leadership of a political party. This was soon belied by his formidable intelligence and steely determination. His almost academic style contrasted with the violence of his language and sentiments. He was sure that, if things went on as they were, his party (ZANU) would emerge as the winners in due course. Their demands, accordingly, were high. They had no intention of losing politically what they had won militarily or of handing power to others who had not done the fighting.

Mugabe seemed to overestimate ZANLA's military capacity, bridling at my suggestion that there was likely to be a high turnout in the April elections: ZANU would persuade the people not to vote. Although he had not abandoned his commitment to elections, he was adamant that these must be preceded by Patriotic Front dominance over the administration and the security forces. This, he acknowledged, the British government had never accepted. Therefore the best course was to get on with the war. Mugabe was scathing at what he regarded as the failure of ZIPRA fully to commit their forces inside Rhodesia. The ZANU leaders, apparently, suspected that Nkomo was holding his forces, with their heavy equipment, in reserve against the possibility of an eventual struggle for power in Salisbury between the nationalist parties, once the whites had gone. Mugabe envisaged elections as a contest between the two wings of the Patriotic Front which, with Shona support, he was convinced he would win.

ZANLA by this time were active over most of the country, up to the outskirts of Salisbury. They remained unable, however, to confront the Rhodesian forces, with their superior firepower, mobility and air support, or to establish any permanently liberated areas. Mugabe's efforts were hampered by his inability to obtain any direct Soviet-bloc military support. The Russians continued to insist on Patriotic Front unity, with Nkomo in the leading role. The East

Germans tried to make condemnation by Mugabe of the Chinese military intervention in Vietnam a condition of their assistance; Mugabe refused. His forces were getting military equipment from the Chinese as well as Mozambicans, Ethiopians and other African countries; but it was much inferior to the equipment being made available by the Russians to ZIPRA. Mugabe was conscious that among African leaders generally he had less support than Nkomo; but the reverse was true within Zimbabwe. The war, he realized, might still be protracted. But his forces had been making steady progress, every year, since 1972. There were now signs of crumbling. Psychologically better prepared than Nkomo for a long struggle, what Mugabe was looking for was something more like the Lusaka agreement, whereby the Portuguese had surrendered Mozambique to Samora Machel, than the Anglo-American proposals. Mugabe's party had developed their own revolutionary philosophy. If they won, they did not look likely to be much interested in checks and balances and arrangements to protect minority rights.

After this uncompromising session, I had lunch on the beach with a young officer in the Embassy, who was our main point of liaison with the ZANU leadership and spent much of his time eating and drinking with them. If we did manage to get another negotiation under way, I wanted to know, how were we going to persuade ZANU to negotiate seriously? How were we going to be able to convince them that this would not be just another round of talks about talks, in which they could procrastinate indefinitely while seeking to intensify the guerrilla campaign?

He supplied the first clue to what might be attempted instead. 'They will not take you seriously', he said, 'until they get to Lancaster House. They know that it is there that the independence constitutions for the other British colonies were decided.' It would be hard enough to get them to negotiate seriously in a formal constitutional conference. They certainly would not do so in any other circumstances.

In Lusaka, I visited Joshua Nkomo in his house adjoining that of his friend and mentor, President Kaunda. Nkomo was a mixture of bluster and charm. There was no sign of a collective leadership here. Nkomo launched into a tirade against the treatment he was receiving in the Western press.

It was indeed forgotten that he had only been driven to take up the armed struggle in 1976, after the failure of numerous efforts to find a negotiated path to majority rule. But he could hardly expect much better so long as he went on celebrating the shooting down of civil aircraft, while his repeated claims of imminent military victory were doing no less damage to his reputation inside Rhodesia. Conscious of the extent to which the political tide had been flowing ZANU's way, Nkomo had been stung by Mugabe's allegations that ZANLA were doing most of the fighting. His prestige would suffer further if ZIPRA failed to make an impact in the election period; but any attempt by his forces to attack with their heavy equipment would be bound to result in heavy losses.

On this visit to Lusaka, I befriended Ariston Chambati, Secretary-General of the Patriotic Front. Along with other moderates in the party, he kept urging Nkomo to keep open the prospect of negotiations. As Chambati confirmed, despite Kaunda's support, the relationship with the Zambians was not an easy one, ZIPRA having failed narrowly to shoot down a couple of Zambian aircraft. Other leaders of his party, particularly those with strong Soviet connections, were encouraging Nkomo to try to present himself as more radical than Mugabe. This group believed in the inevitability of a struggle for power with ZANU. ZIPRA's strategy in that event would be to 'seize the towns', establishing themselves with their heavy equipment in Bulawayo and Salisbury. The moderates considered this an extremely dangerous doctrine. They understood the ebbing of support for Nkomo throughout Mashonaland and that if a negotiating opportunity were not taken, his chances thereafter could fade quickly.

Patriotic Front unity seemed largely a fiction. The pursuit of the Anglo-American proposals had obliged the Patriotic Front to hold meetings to work out common positions. Contacts otherwise were minimal and there was no military co-ordination. Nkomo increasingly was being forced back on his Matabeleland base. Mugabe was showing little interest in negotiating with the whites, still less the internal leaders. The party he and others had created was based on the idea that power had to be won, not negotiated for. He was interested only in the moment at which the whites, under the pressure of military necessity, would agree to surrender power. That day might be some way off, but it would come in the end. Nkomo was more interested in negotiations, but would want to be assured of a pre-eminent position in any negotiated arrangement; and to this neither Muzorewa nor Mugabe would ever agree.

My visit to the region had an unexpected aftermath. The US Air Force plane in which I had travelled to Salisbury was found by the Rhodesians to have photographic surveillance equipment installed in it. They informed the South Africans, who expelled the US Military Attaché and his plane. This clumsy episode was not an auspicious start to the dealings I was going to have to have with the Rhodesian commanders. Flower assured me that he knew this had been done without my knowledge.

A few days later, as if to demonstrate his vulnerability, Rhodesian forces razed to the ground the villa in which I had met Nkomo in Lusaka.

2 A Change of Government

On 28 March 1979 the Labour government lost a vote of confidence in the House of Commons, precipitating an election which, the opinion polls suggested, the Conservative party might win.

Rhodesia was the foreign-policy issue on which the Conservative and Labour parties were furthest apart. Public support had ebbed away from David Owen's apparently hopeless attempts to negotiate a settlement. Ian Smith had always had a considerable following in Britain. The Conservatives had strongly criticized the Labour government for failing to support the internal settlement, offering the hope of evolutionary change. The Conservative party manifesto stated that if the Rhodesian elections fulfilled the proviso that a settlement must be acceptable to the people of Rhodesia as a whole, the next government would have the duty to return Rhodesia to a state of legality, lift sanctions and do its utmost to ensure that the new independent state gained international recognition.

In a speech on 24 March Mrs Thatcher said that the Conservative party, unlike the government, was not prepared to pre-judge the Rhodesian elections. The party spokesman on foreign affairs, Francis Pym, said on 9 April that if the election took place in reasonably free and fair conditions and with a reasonable turnout, the last of the principles which had governed British policy would be satisfied.

One week later, however, Pym introduced some further thoughts. It would not, he said, be possible to make a snap judgement immediately the result of the Rhodesian election was known. 'The whole issue will require full consideration once we have the resources of government behind us. It may also be appropriate to have detailed discussions with our European and American allies and the Commonwealth.' Lord Carrington, the other leading candidate on the Conservative side for the post of Foreign Secretary, said a few days later: 'If we are going to bring Rhodesia back to legality, it will be necessary to get the support and agreement of

the international community.' These successive glosses passed
unnoticed by many at the time.

Mrs Thatcher had chosen to observe the elections on her
behalf a team led by Alan Lennox-Boyd, who had been
Colonial Secretary throughout much of the 1950s. By now
73 years old, immensely tall, unfailingly courteous, he was a
respected figure, of undoubted integrity. He was assisted by
an able and energetic team, including Miles Hudson, who
had served as adviser to Alec Douglas-Home.

I was asked to brief Lord Boyd's team before they went
to Rhodesia. I told them that I thought there would be a
high turnout and that Muzorewa would easily win the elections. With all the white reservists called up for the election period, the Patriotic Front would be unable to disrupt
them. But only one of the three African parties with any
real support – that of Muzorewa – was participating. The
Front had been invited to participate, but under conditions
– control by the Rhodesian army and police – it was known
they would not accept. The war would continue and the
result was unlikely to be recognized by any other African
country.

As, in the Department, we prepared for a possible change
of government, it was clear that the Conservatives would
not be prepared simply to continue the policy of their predecessors towards Rhodesia; nor was this desirable anyway.

I knew nothing of Mrs Thatcher. But it seemed to me
that the argument that we should not recognize the outcome of the elections in Rhodesia because that would anger
the Commonwealth and imperil our shrinking assets elsewhere in Africa was very unlikely to be accepted by her. But
if we did recognize a Muzorewa government which attracted
no other support and then went under, that would do great
damage to Britain's interests and reputation. Mrs Thatcher
seemed more likely to be prepared to consider a bolder
plan which, in any event, was what the by now desperate
circumstances required. This would entail the British government playing a far more direct role, both in deciding the
future constitution and in actually bringing the territory to
independence.

Without Peter Carrington's appointment as Foreign Secretary, there would have been no Rhodesia settlement. Nevertheless, the conclusions he came to at the end of the process were by no means those with which he entered office. The Rhodesia problem, a nemesis of British politicians for 15 years, was familiar to him. He held Ian Smith and the Rhodesian Front in complete disdain. But nor, as he makes clear in his memoirs,* did he have much time for the Patriotic Front, or for the means by which they were seeking to liberate their country. He suspected that Alec Douglas-Home might be correct in suggesting that what they wanted was 'one man, one vote – once'. He felt, like others, that the previous government had done little to encourage Muzorewa and the internal settlement. Muzorewa had emerged the victor in an election which, whatever the blemishes, compared more than favourably with others held in independent Africa. Sanctions had been intended to bring down the Smith regime, not to be used against an African government in Rhodesia; and there was no prospect of the Conservative party renewing them anyway.

So there were very strong pressures to recognize Muzorewa's government forthwith. There was an obvious temptation simply to declare Rhodesia independent, and that Britain no longer had responsibility for it. This would have the merit of being what many regarded as a belated recognition of reality. It also would have been popular, certainly in the Conservative party. Nkomo's blustering performances and Mugabe's public commitment to a Marxist one-party state had done nothing to endear them to British opinion. Nkomo had suffered a series of military reverses. Muzorewa seemed to be the only herbivore in the Rhodesian jungle.

Successive British governments had declared that they would grant legal independence to Rhodesia once the all-important fifth principle – the consent of the majority of the population of Rhodesia – was fulfilled. An election had now taken place in which two-thirds of the African electorate had voted for an African Prime Minister and an African majority in Parliament. Lord Boyd's report was bound to carry great weight with the government and in the Conservative party.

* Peter Carrington, *Reflect on Things Past* (London: Collins, 1988), Chapter 13.

In common with almost all other observers present at the Rhodesian elections, he was known to have formed a favourable judgement on them. The fifth principle looked to many as close to being fulfilled as, in the circumstances prevailing in Rhodesia, it was ever likely to be.

The Conservative government came very close to concluding that it had been fulfilled. It would at the time have required an extraordinary suspension of disbelief to imagine that, one year later, a fresh election would be held under British auspices, with an even higher turnout and a very different result. Lord Boyd's conclusions were announced to the House of Commons on 18 May. They were that the elections had been fairly conducted and were as free as was possible in the circumstances. He also expressed the view that the population had voted in numbers which demonstrated a significant judgement on the constitution; and that, although neither wing of the Patriotic Front had contested the election, 'we think that the result represented the wish of the majority of the electorate of the country however calculated'.

Peter Carrington said that the government would be guided by Lord Boyd's conclusions, but stopped just short of committing himself to the proposition that the fifth principle had been fulfilled.

Carrington faced some difficult decisions, with not much time to decide between them. Ian Smith's determination to remain in the government despite all his earlier hints that he would withdraw had given the kiss of death to Muzorewa's already slim chances of acceptance elsewhere in Africa. Even if Britain did so, other Western governments would not recognize the new regime: they would continue to give priority to their interests elsewhere in Africa. The UN Security Council would not authorize others to lift sanctions; a threat to the peace manifestly would still exist. The war would continue, with every probability of increased Soviet and Cuban involvement.

Carrington was not much impressed by the Commonwealth reactions to the Rhodesian elections, the more so as no Commonwealth government had been represented at them and most were pledged to support the Patriotic Front come what may. But he had no desire to be accused of taking action which could threaten a break-up of the Commonwealth before the Commonwealth heads of government meeting scheduled for Lusaka in August. The British government could not afford to let its Rhodesia policy be dictated from elsewhere in Africa if it were ever to hope to find a way out of the Rhodesian imbroglio; and it accepted that the process of bringing Rhodesia to independence was unlikely to be accomplished without some damage to British interests elsewhere. Clearly, however, it was its duty to limit that damage to the extent it could.

There were, furthermore, some obvious question-marks about the prospects of survival of the hybrid state of Zimbabwe-Rhodesia. The only areas not yet substantially affected by the war were Salisbury and Bulawayo. The death toll in 1978, at nearly 5000, was equal to that of the two previous years combined. The casualty rate in 1979 was likely to be twice that of 1978. The Patriotic Front had no capacity to confront the Rhodesian security forces, but believed they could win a war of attrition. And the tide had been running slowly in their favour. The morale of the white community was crucial; 14 000 had left in the previous year.

The dilemma for the British government was real. It was open to it, instead of declaring Rhodesia independent, simply to choose not to seek parliamentary approval for the continuation of sanctions when Section 2 of the Southern Rhodesia Act fell to be renewed, as it did annually, in November. If Congress obliged the US Administration to lift sanctions, the positions in Britain and the United States would be similar. But a failure to maintain sanctions without a return to legality in Rhodesia would put the government in breach of its obligations under the UN Charter.

There was an obvious danger that this would happen anyway. There were other and worse dangers. If the security situation continued to deteriorate, there was a risk, within two or three years, of a general collapse and the evacuation of the European population in circumstances reminiscent of the last weeks of the Algerian War.

Rhodesia had long been a case of Britain being required to exercise responsibility without power. With a war now in progress it could reasonably be argued that it would be most unwise to get more directly involved. But if the situation deteriorated to the point of collapse – including the possi-

bility of fighting between the two wings of the Patriotic Front
– Britain faced the prospect of having to help evacuate the
140 000 British citizens or persons entitled to claim citizen-
ship in Rhodesia. The Rhodesian forces no doubt would
have been able to hold the key centres and in such circumstances would have got direct support from South Africa.
But there was no low-risk policy in relation to Rhodesia.
The only effective as well as the only honourable form of
disengagement was to find a proper basis for the granting
of legal independence and to give Rhodesia the best start
in the world that could be achieved.

It was apparent that there was no possibility of agreement
on the Anglo-American proposals, and that a new basis for
a settlement would have to be worked out.
So far as the Carter Administration was concerned, however,
the Anglo-American proposals were well-nigh sacrosanct. They
offered a basis on which to maintain a comfortable position
in the international community, to withhold recognition from
the internal settlement and thereby to maintain good relations with other African countries. But they could not contribute to a settlement of the problem either in terms of
the situation in Rhodesia or of Britain's involvement in it.
    That negotiating approach had been based increasingly
on an attempt to devise a plan which would be accepted by
the Patriotic Front – an attempt in which the British and
American negotiators had not been able to succeed, since
Owen in particular was not prepared to give way to all their
demands. It never was clear, as Kaunda put it, who was to
bell the cat – the cat being Ian Smith – and how the Rhodesians were to be brought to surrender power. The impression had been created that the British and American
governments would somehow know how to deliver the internal
parties. Expectations had been aroused that the Anglo-American proposals actually would be implemented. When it became
apparent that they would not, African leaders understand-
ably lost interest in them – except to the extent that they
inhibited the British and American governments from giving
any encouragement to the internal settlement.

The alternative approach was to try to build on the changes which had taken place inside Rhodesia and to seek to carry them forward to a point at which wider acceptance would be achieved. It was too early to say how far that process could be taken, or where precisely it would lead. Carrington was unimpressed by criticism of the Rhodesian elections by governments the bulk of whom had no record of devotion to free elections themselves. But he was convinced that to have any prospect of success, and of limiting damage to British interests, the government must seek to obtain a measure at least of international support. It was obvious that this was no less essential if the people of Rhodesia themselves were to have any prospect of a better future, and of an end to or a winding-down of the war.

On examining the Zimbabwe-Rhodesia constitution, Carrington came to the same conclusion as his advisers, namely that it was like no other constitution on the basis of which Britain had granted independence to a former colony. No less of a hybrid than the name of the new state, it manifestly was designed to keep the main levers of power, including control over the armed forces, police, civil service and judiciary, in the hands of the whites. Carrington concluded that it would be very difficult to justify granting legal independence on this basis.

The first task for the new British government was to get itself into a position to exert some influence in Salisbury. Security Council resolutions passed at the request of the Wilson government had prohibited UN member states from maintaining diplomatic or consular representatives in Rhodesia, to avoid a process of creeping recognition. As a result Britain had maintained no permanent representation in Rhodesia since 1969, thereby cutting itself off from any direct means of bringing influence to bear. Instead successive governments had tried to operate through intermediaries, not always with very happy results, and through visits by officials.

With Rhodesia at the top of the British government's foreign policy priorities, this was an absurd state of affairs. The UN resolutions notwithstanding, the gap needed filling and David

Owen would himself have taken steps to fill it if he had remained as Foreign Secretary.

Sir Antony Duff, the Deputy Under-Secretary and senior Foreign Office official responsible for Africa, was despatched to make contact with Muzorewa. A most unusual official, Duff belonged to a school and generation which believed that it was Britain's role not just to observe and, most often, deplore the state of the world, but to do something about it. A former naval officer, who had distinguished himself during the war, he combined personal authority, good humour and a certain steeliness of spirit in measures calculated to impress both white and black Rhodesians, as they did Carrington and Mrs Thatcher. Sir Antony's contribution to the eventual resolution of the Rhodesia problem was as great as that of any other person, certainly on the British side.

Duff assured Muzorewa of the Conservative government's intention to work with him to find a solution. But he emphasized the need to bring the war to an end and achieve maximum acceptance in Africa. Muzorewa had hoped for immediate recognition. He harboured illusions that a number of other African countries might recognize him, even with Ian Smith in his government. But he accepted that the Conservative government was offering a new approach. He was told that the British government would be sending a senior official to Salisbury to maintain contact with him.

Cyrus Vance, meanwhile, had arrived in London to meet Carrington. The Americans remained attached to the Anglo-American proposals. They feared that the Conservative government would move towards recognition of the internal settlement and the effect this could have in Congress, where their own policy was under attack, and on their relations with the rest of Africa.

So far as the British were concerned, it was central to the new approach that this should be a purely British initiative and not an Anglo-American enterprise. This was partly from necessity: the attitude of the Conservative government to the problem was very different from that of the Carter Administration. It was Carter who had rendered the Anglo-American proposals non-negotiable by accepting Nyerere's demand that the future army should be 'based on the liberation forces'.

The interminable processes, furthermore, which had been involved in consultations on the Anglo-American proposals had proved liable to result in an incapacity to take any action at all. The US officials principally concerned saw an eventual Patriotic Front victory as inevitable and were determined that the United States should be seen to be on the side of the progressive forces in Africa. The Administration, they freely admitted, was no less influenced by its desire to keep on terms with the black caucus in Congress. They did succeed in improving greatly US relations with much of black Africa, which had reached a nadir with Henry Kissinger's support for the South African intervention in Angola. But the Africans could not readily understand the failure of a superpower to *do* something about Rhodesia, and tended to conclude that it did not really want to. The United States would be inclined to continue to give priority to their interests elsewhere in Africa; and few, apart from the Rhodesians, could blame them for that. But the urgency of the problem from Britain's point of view was too great to continue on this basis.

It was important, however, to try to secure adequate US understanding for the policy now being developed in London. After two days of discussion with Carrington, Vance agreed, with undisguised relief, that Britain should take the lead. But he and his advisers did contribute to the development of British policy. Carrington told him that the government had to honour the undertakings in the Conservative manifesto. There was no prospect of renewing sanctions in November. The Americans feared that this would alienate black Africa and increase Cuban and Soviet influence. Reflecting discussions between British and US officials, Vance speculated about the possibility of some revision of the constitution; an attempt to move the Salisbury government towards an all-party conference; and elections under some form of international supervision.

The British government by this time had made a series of statements about its approach. In the debate on the Queen's speech on 15 May, Mrs Thatcher said that it was the government's intention to build on the changes which had taken place in Rhodesia to achieve a return to legality in conditions that secured wide international recognition.

There would be consultations with the Commonwealth and other Western governments. 'We must and will take into account the wider international implications. ... we intend to proceed with vigour to resolve the issue.'

It was a promise not many believed the British government capable of keeping. Carrington told the House of Lords that it was Britain's responsibility to try to bring Rhodesia to independence in conditions which offered the people of that country the prospect of a more peaceful future. The need to win some international support was at least as great for Rhodesia as for Britain.

If others failed to understand this coded language, it was well enough understood in Salisbury. The *Rhodesia Herald* commented that it might have been thought that all Rhodesia had to do was to await Lord Boyd's report and recognition. 'Unfortunately events were never likely to be as simple as that.'

In Salisbury on 1 June the Muzorewa government at last was installed, more than a month after the elections. Ian Smith said that after 15 years as Prime Minister, he had no regrets. He was still opposed to black majority rule. He believed that it had come too soon.

Muzorewa in speeches across the country had contended that the elections would bring peace, as the guerrillas would realize that the internal leaders had won what they had been fighting for. Such expectations never looked like being fulfilled. The guerrillas, forced to lie low during the period of maximum Rhodesian deployment, resumed their activities as soon as the elections were over. A record 891 people were killed inside the country in May. The internal leaders continued to fight among themselves.

On 7 June President Carter announced the decision he was required by Congress to make on the continuation of sanctions. He stated that he was convinced that the best interests of the United States would not be served by lifting sanctions. The Zimbabwe-Rhodesia constitution was designed to preserve white control. It had not been voted on by the African electorate. The Patriotic Front had not been able to participate. He considered that to lift sanctions would be contrary to international law and damaging to US interests in Africa.

3 Lusaka

The next move was to find an envoy on behalf of the Conservative government to consult the African presidents. The best candidate looked to be David Harlech. Best-known as the British Ambassador in Washington and friend of President Kennedy, he had served as deputy leader of the Pearce Commission which, in 1972, had concluded that the Smith–Home proposals were not acceptable to the African population. This, we hoped, should help to establish his credibility with the African leaders with whom he would have to deal.

David Harlech visited southern Africa in June 1979 accompanied by my deputy, Peter Barlow, who helped him with his report. As Margaret Thatcher recalls, she was not at all keen that he should talk to Nkomo and Mugabe: 'their forces had carried out atrocities which disgusted everyone and I was as keen to avoid dealing with terrorists abroad as I would be at home. However, unpleasant realities had to be faced.'* Mrs Thatcher was persuaded that Harlech should meet them, as well as the Commonwealth African presidents, President Machel of Mozambique, Muzorewa and Ian Smith.

David Harlech found that none of the African governments would give even tacit support if Britain granted Rhodesia independence on the basis of the *status quo*. This applied to the supposedly 'moderate' Presidents Banda of Malawi and Seretse Khama of Botswana no less than to the others. He found a general sentiment that a settlement must be seen to be British and not merely the legalization of a solution which Britain, the colonial power, had played no part in working out.

At this point the South African Foreign Minister, Pik Botha, arrived in London. The South African government at this time were developing the notion of a constellation of neighbouring states with close economic ties to South Africa and well-disposed African governments. Rhodesia, Botswana and eventually Namibia, it was hoped, would conform to this pattern.

* Margaret Thatcher, *The Downing Street Years* (London: HarperCollins, 1993), pp. 72–3.

Pik Botha was one of the most 'enlightened' (*verligte*) members of the South African government, but that was not saying much at the time. He gave Peter Carrington and his deputy, Ian Gilmour, a 45-minute lecture on the iniquity of Western policy in southern Africa, alleging constant moving of the goalposts and allowing precious little time for reply. Bent on revenge, I telephoned 10 Downing Street to ensure that when Pik Botha saw the Prime Minister, she gave *him* a 45-minute lecture in return.

Margaret Thatcher then set off for Australia, where she said at a press conference that sanctions would lapse in November and it was doubtful if there would be a majority in Parliament to renew them. This provoked a tremendous outcry.

Harlech's report convinced the government that they would have to insist on changes to the Rhodesian constitution. Through this recommendation David Harlech, before his tragic death in a car crash, rendered his country a service as great as any he had in his political career.

In July, Bishop Muzorewa visited Washington. President Carter and Cyrus Vance told him that he must work with the British to achieve a settlement. In London, the Prime Minister and Peter Carrington assured him of their support for what had been achieved, but insisted that the independence constitution would have to be approved by the British Parliament and must be comparable to those established in other cases. Muzorewa was assured that if others opposed a settlement the British government regarded as reasonable, it would be prepared to proceed anyway.

Muzorewa's attempts to win support elsewhere in Africa were getting nowhere. President Tolbert of Liberia, a somewhat unlikely representative of 'progressive' opinion, and himself soon to be killed in a coup in his own country, banned Muzorewa's representatives from the meeting of the Organization of African Unity in Monrovia. The Patriotic Front leaders refused to have anything to do with him. 'War is better than negotiations', proclaimed Nkomo.

Nor were things going well inside Rhodesia. Hardly any of the guerrillas defected to the government which, instead, recruited large numbers of 'auxiliaries', whom Walls himself described as urban riff-raff. The Rhodesian forces tried belatedly to bring them under control. In one incident pro-Sithole auxiliaries refused to be disarmed. The Rhodesian army opened fire, killing 183 auxiliaries, with no casualties to the security forces. This put an end to Sithole's private army. Muzorewa said that they had been guilty of murder, abduction, rape, house-breaking, theft and extortion – all of which no doubt was true, but left some questions as to why they had been permitted to operate in the first place.

Following his visit to London, it looked as if Muzorewa could be brought to acquiesce in constitutional change, though there was certain to be fierce resistance from Ian Smith and the Rhodesian Front. The idea was to publish outline constitutional proposals immediately after the Commonwealth Conference in Lusaka, with invitations to Muzorewa, Nkomo and Mugabe to attend a constitutional conference at Lancaster House in London in September.

Wishing to retain the element of surprise, Margaret Thatcher kept her cards close to her chest as she set off to the Conference in Lusaka. The approach to the meeting could hardly have been less auspicious. The other heads of government all were convinced of her intention to recognize Muzorewa. Zambia, including its capital, for months had been treated as a free-fire zone by the Rhodesian army and air force. As the RAF VC10 neared Lusaka, Peter Carrington asked the Prime Minister why she was donning dark glasses. Mrs Thatcher feared that, on arrival, acid might be thrown in her eyes.*

The British delegates arrived to a very mixed welcome. The atmosphere initially was far from promising. But Zambia and Botswana were suffering desperately from the war. For Tanzania, Julius Nyerere's main concern was to ensure that Mrs Thatcher did not recognize the Muzorewa government.

The discussion on Rhodesia, expected to be stormy, opened with a skilful and moderate speech by Nyerere. What was

---

* Peter Carrington, *Reflect on Things Past* (London: Collins, 1988), Chapter 12.

required in Rhodesia, he argued, was a genuinely democratic constitution and elections in which all parties could
participate.

Mrs Thatcher, in response, developed a rather similar argument. The international community, she said, had lost
few opportunities to remind Britain that it was its responsibility to bring Rhodesia to legal independence. Britain had
every intention of discharging that responsibility. It would
do so on the same basis as for other dependent territories.
The British government would be making proposals which
would be put to all the parties.

These speeches opened the way for agreement in Lusaka.
The Commonwealth Secretary-General, Sonny Ramphal,
played the main part in helping to work out the communiqué.
To the fury of the British delegates, the contents were leaked
in advance by the Australian Prime Minister, Malcolm Fraser,
who despite or perhaps because of his conservative domestic policies kept trying to position himself some distance
to the left of the Patriotic Front. The communiqué recognized that it was Britain's responsibility to bring Zimbabwe
to legal independence; that the existing constitution was de-
fective, though there should be safeguards for minorities;
and that the independence government must be chosen
through free elections supervised under British government
authority, with Commonwealth observers present.

Mrs Thatcher and Carrington had decided to call a constitutional conference, and to invite the Patriotic Front to
it, before ever setting off for Lusaka. The new and crucial
element at Lusaka, however, was the commitment to new
elections, under British supervision. Nyerere had played a
helpful role, not least because he still feared that Britain
might recognize Muzorewa. Muzorewa already had been told
that, if the independence constitution were agreed, there
would have to be a test of acceptability. But the British government hitherto had not committed itself to fresh elections,
or to organizing these itself.

In taking that step the Conservative government had been
persuaded to go back to the principle underlying the Anglo-
American proposals – that of impartially supervised elections,
which alone afforded the prospect of avoiding a fight to
the finish in Rhodesia.

In Salisbury, Muzorewa pointed out that Lord Boyd had concluded that the April elections had been free and fair. There was no reason whatever for new elections to be held. There also was a strong reaction from the South Africans, who insisted that if the Muzorewa government were not recognized forthwith, Rhodesia would be in danger of imminent collapse. These alarmist reports were partly attributable to a Rhodesian tendency, in their contacts with the South Africans, to exaggerate their difficulties in order to secure additional financial and military support.

Before leaving Lusaka, Mrs Thatcher told the press that the problem was to find a solution which would bring an end to the hostilities. If Britain had acted alone this would not have been of much help to Rhodesia. Asked if Britain would provide troops to supervise the elections, Mrs Thatcher replied that she did not anticipate any British troops going to Rhodesia. She refused to speculate about the possibility of a short period of direct British rule. But it would be culpable not to make the attempt to bring an end to the war. The Conservative government, she argued, had not executed a *volte-face*. It had said from the outset that it must do its utmost to ensure that the new independent state gained international recognition.

In the Department, the way was now open for us to put forward our constitutional proposals. These were based on a comparison with other independence constitutions. There were precedents for the special representation of minority communities in Parliament for a period after independence in Tanzania, Zambia and Kenya – but not for the blocking power and stranglehold on most new legislation given to the whites under the Zimbabwe-Rhodesia constitution. There also were precedents for the protection of basic human rights any challenge to which could be referred to the courts – though the courts in a number of countries since independence had done little or proved powerless to uphold them.

Adopting a technique which was to be used in each stage of the Lancaster House Conference, we decided to put forward the proposals in the first instance in outline form. They provided that for a period after independence a minority of seats in Parliament would be reserved for the white electorate. But the minority representatives alone would not have a power of veto over legislation not affecting basic human rights. These proposals, worked out before the Lusaka conference, made clear the British government's determination that the new constitution should provide for genuine majority rule. Muzorewa and the Patriotic Front were invited to bring delegations to a constitutional Conference at Lancaster House in September.

Fundamental to this strategy was the idea that *agreement must first be reached on the independence constitution*. This was the opposite of what had been attempted in most previous negotiating efforts, where efforts had been made to get agreement on power-sharing arrangements and merging the rival armies and otherwise seek to deal with everything except the fundamental problem, which was the attainment of genuine majority rule. If agreement could be reached on the constitution, we reasoned, then the war would be reduced to a competition for power between the parties which, instead, could be coerced into settling it in elections under impartial control.

To avoid a re-run of the previous sterile and interminable 'talks about talks', the British team decided that acceptance of the independence constitution should be made a precondition for the subsequent discussions on its implementation. Nkomo and Mugabe were rejecting any cease-fire in advance of a settlement, the idea of special representation for the white community and Britain's responsibility for fresh elections. But, under pressure from the Commonwealth African leader, they agreed to attend the Conference.

President Nyerere said that Britain should not approach the Conference as a neutral arbitrating between the contending groups. It should act as the decolonizing power. Posing the most vital question of all, he wondered how Britain could secure sufficient real authority on the ground to supervise elections. He was told by Mrs Thatcher that Britain did indeed intend to act as the decolonizing power and would be looking for support from others as it took the steps to do so.

4 Lancaster House

As the Conference convened, veterans of Rhodesia negotiations looked on more in pity than in hope. Few saw much reason to believe that it would not turn into another in the apparently unending series of initiatives that flourished briefly before leading nowhere. The British team had to work out a strategy to prevent that happening.

In all previous negotiations the Patriotic Front had insisted on control over the administration and the security forces before elections were held. If they maintained that position at Lancaster House, no agreement would be possible. If Muzorewa accepted the British proposals and the Patriotic Front did not, there would be no option but to proceed with the internal parties – the so-called second-class solution. This would have posed obvious and serious risks. It most certainly was not the preferred solution. But if this last, and most determined, attempt at a settlement failed, there would be nothing to be gained by preserving the fiction of Britain's responsibility for Rhodesia. The time would have come to bring that fiction to an end.

The Rhodesians were pinning their hopes on the lifting of sanctions in November, but it was difficult to see how this could have much effect on the security situation. The military commanders were aware that time was not on their side and that white emigration and the lowering of white morale, inadequate equipment and a declining economy put them on the losing side in the long term. Subsequent protestations by some of the Rhodesian commanders that they were 'let down', by Britain, that they could have got on top of the security situation or that the lifting of sanctions by Britain alone could have made a real impact on it should be seen in the light of their own estimate at the time that they were losing the war. This trend could only have been reversed or contained by massive external military assistance – or a weakening of support for the Front by some at least of the neighbouring states and on the part of the local population.

This did not mean that the Rhodesians had no option but to agree to whatever the British proposed. This was never how the negotiations appeared at the time. They had given sufficient demonstrations of their capacity to reject negotiated solutions whatever the consequences for them. They could still try to force the partial lifting of sanctions in November by Britain and the US Congress and to get the South Africans more heavily committed to their support – and despite periodic threats to cut their losses, the South Africans at this time were increasing their military involvement. It also was open to the Rhodesians to raise the stakes in the war. This they were doing by carrying out increasingly unrestrained raids on the neighbouring countries. Before the April elections they had launched a series of successful attacks on guerrilla camps in Zambia and Mozambique and had attacked for the first time a ZIPRA camp in Angola. In March they organized the demolition of the oil-depot in Beira. In April Rhodesian commandos destroyed the ZIPRA headquarters in Lusaka.

Raids into Zambia were resumed in August. A massive Rhodesian attack was launched to destroy strategic and economic targets in Mozambique just before the Conference opened. This succeeded in inflicting great damage on what was left of Mozambique's economy, but proved costly also for the Rhodesians, who lost 11 men when a helicopter was shot down. The Rhodesians continued and intensified attacks on strategic targets in the neighbouring countries throughout the Conference.

Nor would it have been wise to underestimate Ian Smith's capacity once again to destroy the chances of a settlement. We concluded that this did *not* mean that we should be prepared to make concessions to him. It would have been extremely damaging to permit the constitutional changes we were seeking to be whittled away or engage in a process of haggling about them. We had to be ready *vis-à-vis* both the other delegations to lay down clearly what Britain could accept and then to stick to it. These tactics would require a display of political courage and determination, as Ian Smith sought to push the government up against the sanctions deadline and threatened to use the blocking power of the Rhodesian Front MPs to veto changes he disliked. There being no prospect of persuading Ian Smith to agree to the changes we were proposing, the only way to counter his influence was to aim to isolate him within his own delegation.

Real power on the Rhodesian side rested with the military commanders. Their representatives at the Conference were Ken Flower, the head of the Rhodesian Central Intelligence Organization, and Air Vice-Marshal Harold Hawkins, the Rhodesian representatives in South Africa. Over dinner at the Hyde Park Hotel, Tony Duff and I explained the constitutional changes on which we would be insisting. They reacted calmly enough to these. It was clear, however, that they were thinking in terms of a settlement with Britain, not with the Patriotic Front. They made clear that the breaking-point for the commanders would be any interference with the structure of their forces before elections were held.

We knew from our contacts with the Patriotic Front that they saw it as in their interests to string out the Conference. They did not expect anything positive to emerge and suspected that it was a device by the Conservative government to enable them to recognize Muzorewa.

The British team had to work out a strategy to prevent it turning into a re-run of the fiasco three years earlier in Geneva. Then a conference had been held under the chairmanship of the Labour government's Ambassador to the United Nations, Ivor Richard. In the two months of its existence, no serious negotiation was ever engaged. The Patriotic Front objected to the presence of the Rhodesian representatives except as part of the British delegation; to the chairmanship of Ivor Richard (instead of the Foreign Secretary); and to the hotel expenses provided by the British government for their delegates. Ian Smith refused to negotiate on any basis other than acceptance of an agreement which he had worked out with Henry Kissinger. None of the African delegations was prepared to accept white Rhodesian control over the police and army, which was part of that agreement. The main business was devoted to a meaningless argument about the date for independence. After two weeks, Ian Smith left. With a change of Administration pending in the United States, Kissinger was unable to do anything to retrieve the situation. The meeting adjourned in December, never to be reconvened.

The Rhodesia Department by this time had been reinforced with the arrival of Charles Powell. We had joined the Foreign Office on the same day and become the firmest of friends. He combined qualities of intelligence, imagination and determination rare in any bureaucracy, anywhere.

On the eve of the Conference, Charles and I called on Joshua Nkomo, installed with his delegation at the Royal Garden Hotel in Kensington. Nkomo protested at the paltry allowances his delegation were receiving – insufficient, he said, to pay for a decent meal. To persuade him otherwise, Charles and I offered to take him to the very modest restaurant in the Fulham Road we were intending to eat at after we saw him. Amidst much hilarity, this offer was declined and we heard no more on the subject of allowances.

On the morning the Conference was due to open we faced the expected next test. We were informed by the Patriotic Front that they would refuse to attend unless Muzorewa and his colleagues were declared to be part of the British delegation, sitting on our side of the table. We replied that the Conference would open that afternoon with whoever chose to attend it and the table arrangements would remain as they were. Nkomo and Mugabe duly appeared and no more was heard of this suggestion.

And so the Conference began beneath the chandeliers and amid the gilt and tapestries of Lancaster House. In his opening statement, Peter Carrington said that the people assembled in the conference room had it in their power to end the war. Neither side had infinite resources. The independence constitution was the fundamental issue. If that could be resolved, the British government would play its part in bringing it into effect.

Muzorewa argued that elections had already been held: it was the duty of the British government to grant independence and lift sanctions. Nkomo and Mugabe wanted to settle who would exercise power during elections before discussing the constitution. Carrington ruled that the constitution must be agreed first. The British then would make proposals for the administration of the country before elections. This entailed overruling Muzorewa as well as the Patriotic Front. At the same time, we published detailed proposals for changes to the constitution. Mugabe and Nkomo remained intensely suspicious. But they had begun to be convinced that, this time, the British were serious.

It was clear that if we did not give a determined lead, the Conference would get nowhere. Neither side was prepared to negotiate with the other. There was no prospect of achieving agreement by the normal processes of dialogue or even of mediation between them. The British delegation were determined to retain the initiative by putting forward their own proposals at each stage, and insisting on a response to them; dealing firmly with Ian Smith; adopting throughout the role of *arbitrator*, rather than simply chairman of the Conference; and making clear that, this time, the British government intended to carry out what it proposed.

This last point was by far the most important. The Rhodesians and the Patriotic Front alike had got into the habit of believing that Britain was capable of making proposals, but incapable of acting; and was indeed concerned to avoid assuming direct responsibility, with all the attendant dangers.

So we devised a strategy which consisted of ourselves trying to draw the line on which agreement could in theory be reached: and then trying to push Muzorewa's delegation into acceptance of it *so that whatever was on offer in the conference was a real offer, capable of being implemented.* This meant that the main battles with Muzorewa and his team had to be fought in private. These were every bit as difficult as the battles that subsequently had to be engaged, more publicly, with the Patriotic Front. We were conscious throughout that, contrary to appearances and the impression of the press, it is never as difficult to reach agreement with a liberation movement as it is *to persuade those who hold power to relinquish it.*

We did not proceed on the assumption that a comprehensive settlement was likely to be attainable. It would have been foolhardy to do so. The positions of the parties appeared irreconcilable on all the major issues. Muzorewa needed a settlement, but the Rhodesian reactions to ideas of constitutional change showed that there was tough bargaining ahead – the more so as the British delegation intended to put forward radical proposals and to stick to them. For the Patriotic Front, Nkomo was under more pressure to settle than Mugabe. For him the Conference might well be the last chance; but he was unlikely to settle without Mugabe. The question was whether he might pull ZANU towards a settlement, or whether ZANU would pull him away from one. For Mugabe was making clear that he did not consider that he needed a settlement. Nor was there any reason at this stage for him to believe that one was on offer. Nothing had happened to shake his conviction that genuine majority rule, by which he meant the victory of ZANU, could only be achieved by the armed struggle.

The proceedings were interrupted for tea. We were determined to try to force the delegations to mingle with each other. Many members of the Front and of Muzorewa's delegation had been, at one time or another, in the same party. Others had been at school together. They were going to have to live together if the enterprise was to succeed. These efforts were only partially successful. To the end the atmosphere between the African delegates remained bitter and uneasy. Nkomo and Mugabe regarded Muzorewa and his associates as quislings.

From the outset, however, they had a different attitude to the white members of the Salisbury delegation whom they regarded, rightly, as being still in charge and as representing real power and control over the Rhodesian forces, for whom they had a considerable respect. On the first afternoon the flabbergasted delegates were surprised to see Josaiah Tongogara, the commander of ZANLA, greeting Ian Smith and asking about his mother, who was still living on her farm near Selukwe. Tongogara had grown up on Smith's mother's farm: she had given him sweets as a child. This had not had much effect on his political opinions. Tongogara had shown himself to be a ruthless guerrilla commander; and, like the Rhodesians, he was fighting a bitter war with all the means at his disposal. But when he said he was no racist, Tongogara meant it.

The incident epitomized an intangible element, but one which was to be crucial for the future, causing some of us to believe that the prospects for a solution were not hopeless in Rhodesia, contrary to most of the evidence at the time. The element was the fact that, although the whites committed every possible political crime, including that of blind stupidity, in their efforts to hold on to power, relations at the personal level between black and white never seemed to have broken down irretrievably in Rhodesia. Of course there were plenty of exceptions to this rule, no less among the guerrillas than the Rhodesian Front. Yet in many cases men who had been imprisoned for years without good reason did not seem to emerge from captivity or exile thirsting for personal as distinct from political revenge.

5 Brinkmanship

It was clear that Ian Smith and others intended to try to push the British government up against the deadline for the renewal of sanctions in November, while rejecting any constitutional change or seeking to settle for purely cosmetic amendments. A counter to this ploy had been worked out. It fell to me to explain to the Rhodesians that not all sanctions depended on the Southern Rhodesia Act, which they knew was unlikely to be renewed in November. A wide range of measures existed under other legislation, and these required positive, not merely negative, action to terminate them. While there might be no majority in Parliament for the renewal of sanctions, there would be no majority for their removal either, unless there was an agreement with Britain in the mean time. This was regarded by Ian Smith as another example of British perfidy. Such pressures, unfortunately, were necessary if his resistance was to be overcome – or rather, isolated.

For that, at this stage, was what the negotiation was about. The British delegation benefited greatly from the fact that Ian Smith was no longer in control. But, at the outset, he continued to exert an hypnotic influence over other members of the delegation, who were afraid of him. He continued also to exert a considerable fascination on British opinion. Cheered by the airport workers on his arrival at Heathrow, he drew more cheers at the Battle of Britain memorial service in Westminster Abbey. Fêted by the right wing of the Conservative party, he was courted also by right-wing Senators like Jesse Helms in the United States.

The first month of the Conference was devoted to breaking his hold on the Salisbury delegation. A succession of British governments had underestimated Ian Smith. We were determined not to make the same mistake.

The African members of Muzorewa's delegation were in favour of the British proposals, though some were afraid to say so. Muzorewa was worried that change might cause Rhodesia's military leaders, on whom he depended for his survival, to withdraw their support. Tony Duff and I spent many long hours with his principal advisers – his deputy Silas Mundawarara and James Kamusikiri, head of his private office. While defending Muzorewa's interests, both distinguished themselves throughout the Conference by their concern for the future of their country. Harold Hawkins and Ken Flower represented what was by now the real power in Rhodesia, namely the National Joint Operations Command – the Rhodesian army, air force and police commanders. They did not give the impression that General Walls and the others would frustrate constitutional change.

That left the Rhodesian Front. David Smith, as Finance Minister, more than anyone was conscious of the need for a settlement. He knew that the limit of Rhodesia's resources had been reached, and that there could be no recovery of the economy without a de-escalation of the war. There were limits to South African support. But he never had been known to stand up to Ian Smith, the incontestable leader of his party. Would he do so now?

A revolt was long overdue. But the choice, even at this stage, was not as self-evident as it might seem. All previous revolts against Ian Smith had been crushed with ease, and the rebels consigned not just to political oblivion but subjected also to personal vilification and, in the closed world of white Rhodesian society, a degree of social ostracism. But David Smith knew that this time there would be no second chances and that Ian Smith could offer no alternatives. Peter Carrington saw him privately to tell him that it was now or never. Hawkins and Flower did much to stiffen his determination. In the first breakthrough of the Conference, Muzorewa's delegation announced their acceptance of the main points of the British constitutional proposals. The decision was taken by 11 votes to one, with David Smith in favour and Ian Smith alone dissenting.

Separate meetings continued, meanwhile, with the Patriotic Front. When Carrington announced that 20 seats would be reserved for the whites for some years in the new Parliament, he got a muted reaction from Mugabe who understood that, on their own, the white representatives would have no general veto power.

As the constitution was revised clause by clause, in the

tense atmosphere a tragedy occurred as a young Rhodesian lawyer killed himself at Lancaster House. The Conference was turning into a test of the stamina of all three delegations. Nkomo, complaining about Carrington's 'dictatorial' approach, asked if the outcome was going to be presented on a take-it-or-leave-it basis. He was told that, in effect, it was. Otherwise the discussions would go on forever.

On 3 October we tabled the independence constitution the British government intended to recommend to Parliament. The other delegations were given until 8 October to respond. Muzorewa announced his acceptance. Ian Smith left forthwith for Salisbury to appeal to white opinion there. The British proposals, he said, were the worst offered by any British government since UDI. That, from his point of view, was true, but did little to explain why he had rejected what was on offer before and still less to recognize the straits Rhodesia, thanks to his policies, was in.

From London, Mundawarara replied: 'We are trying here to sort out the mess he has created in our country.' Hawkins and Flower were determined that, this time, Ian Smith should not be permitted to destroy the chance of a settlement with Britain. The decisive voice was that of General Walls, who told Ian Smith that he intended to support Muzorewa.

Nkomo and Mugabe still had not produced their reply. While this was awaited, we intensified our efforts to get the Muzorewa government to agree to fresh elections. This was the key to international acceptance, as well as offering the only hope of an end to the war. Most of the African members of the delegation, who had supported constitutional change, had no enthusiasm for a new electoral contest. But Mundawarara and Kamusikiri understood that without new elections, there would be no settlement.

After days of agonizing, Muzorewa sided with them, declaring furthermore that under the old constitution he was indeed a pawn. In announcing his intention, Muzorewa reminded his delegation that it was he who had most to lose: manifestly, there could be no certainty that he would win fresh elections. The decision again was taken against the opposition of Ian Smith.

At the same time efforts were made in contacts outside the Conference by Carrington's deputy, Ian Gilmour, and by the rest of us to convince Nkomo and Mugabe that we were trying for a settlement in which they could participate. Nkomo was more receptive than Mugabe, who remained deeply suspicious of British intentions. At one meeting Charles Powell and I had with Nkomo at his hotel, his secretary came in bearing an urgent message. She fell to her knees, before presenting it to Nkomo. Ariston Chambati, Secretary-General of the Patriotic Front, told us, laughing, as we left that if we wished to create the right impression at the Foreign Office, we should need to arrange for my own formidable secretary to do the same.

The Conference adjourned for a day to enable Peter Carrington to address the Conservative party conference in Blackpool. It was an occasion as important as any in his political career. He had to carry his party with him along the course now chosen, and which many members of the party, left to their own devices, certainly would not have chosen themselves. While the criticism so far was muted, Carrington was under no illusions as to the opinions of the right wing. Although undoubtedly respected, he was by no means universally popular, as later events were to demonstrate. He appeared at times to be more admired outside than within the Conservative party. Yet Carrington's good humour and keen wit concealed a steeliness of character which was apparent to the other delegations at Lancaster House.

If Carrington left for Blackpool with some anxieties, he need not have worried. His speech there was a triumph. It also was used to warn the Patriotic Front that they must make up their minds. If Britain had acted alone to recognize Muzorewa's government, Carrington told his party, no one would have followed. There would have been no chance of ending the war. But Lancaster House could not be allowed to become a repetition of the empty haggling of Geneva. There must now be a decision on the constitution. It was not feasible to integrate the armed forces or to make other radical changes before elections were held. The time for the lifting of sanctions could not now be far off. No one would be allowed to decide unilaterally that Rhodesia must continue in illegality and isolation. 'What we are striving to do is to solve a tragic problem with honour, with dignity and with justice.' In her speech on the following day, Margaret Thatcher emphasized Britain's duty to do everything in its power to bring an end to a war now rendered pointless by the attainment of genuine majority rule.

There were by this time strong indications that Nkomo and his party were anxious to come to an agreement and that most of the African presidents felt that the British proposals should be accepted. The Front's objections had been whittled down largely to the question of land. The British were not prepared to finance a fund to buy out white farmers, as Julius Nyerere was suggesting. What was required for food production in Rhodesia was to keep European farmers there, not to encourage them to leave, to allow time for African commercial farming to develop. Otherwise Zimbabwe quickly would find itself in the same economic straits as Tanzania. The Commonwealth Secretary-General, Sonny Ramphal, and the US Administration both sought to take a hand. Carrington offered Mugabe and Nkomo an opening, pointing out that the new constitution provided for the acquisition of under-utilized land and promising that Britain would be prepared to help with funds for agricultural development and in seeking to attract international assistance. The US Ambassador, Kingman Brewster, told them that the Americans also would help with land development.

The olive branch seemed at first to have been rejected. Nkomo sought to move on to the next phase of the Conference while reserving the Front's position on the issues of land, pensions, the army, civil service and judiciary.

Carrington adjourned the Conference briefly in an effort to obtain a clear statement from Mugabe and Nkomo that they could accept the independence constitution. When they declined to do so, he said that they were maintaining reservations on issues of major importance. He had tried to help them on the question of land. But the negotiations must proceed step by step if they were not to prove as fruitless as those in Geneva. The British government could not accept the reservations in Nkomo's statement. To do so would mean that major questions would be re-opened after discussion of the interim arrangements. When the Conference resumed, this would be to discuss the arrangements for implementing the independence constitution. Before then he needed to know whether the Front could accept the constitution. It was essential to obtain an unequivocal response to give the Conference a firm basis on which to proceed. For otherwise, if issues could be re-opened at each stage, the discussions would become as circular and self-defeating as in all the previous meetings. The chances of success of the British approach depended on the independence constitution being settled before the Conference went on to discuss the still more difficult issues of the transitional arrangements. It was no less important to maintain the confidence of those who had agreed. Muzorewa, under pressure from those members of his delegation who did not at all relish the thought of fresh elections, was threatening to leave for Salisbury. His anxieties were increased by Ian Smith's campaign in Salisbury to win the support of the Rhodesian Front MPs for his opposition to the British proposals.

In a final effort to force Nkomo and Mugabe over this hurdle – and to keep Muzorewa's delegation at the Conference – Carrington announced that in view of the Patriotic Front's failure to accept the constitution, discussions about the arrangements to implement it would take place without their participation. They would be welcome to join them as soon as they could indicate acceptance of the constitution. It remained the British objective to work out pre-independence arrangements which would enable all parties to participate in free elections.

On the following day, meetings were held with Muzorewa's delegation to discuss the pre-independence arrangements. Carrington was determined to do nothing that would exclude Patriotic Front participation. On 17 October he started to unveil British plans for the transition. The proposals were controversial enough for leaks to be inevitable. That evening the BBC carried a report that Carrington had proposed that a British Governor should assume responsibility in Rhodesia. The Front thus were made aware of the British intention to make radical proposals in the next phase of the Conference.

The Commonwealth Secretary-General criticized Carrington

for proceeding without the Front: this, he contended, was contrary to the Lusaka agreement. But Ramphal also busied himself with seeking a formula that would enable Mugabe and Nkomo to agree; and this time his efforts were successful. On 18 October they produced a statement that if they were satisfied about the vital issues in the pre-independence arrangements, there would not be a need to revert to discussion on the constitution. This enabled the Conference to move on to the next stage of its work against the background of a solid achievement – agreement on the independence constitution. That achievement increased the expectation of success in the next and still more difficult stage. The tactics adopted over the constitution – the struggle to win the agreement of the Muzorewa delegation, the gradual elaboration of the British proposals and their defence against significant amendment by *either* side, with a time limit (somewhat elastic, but real) for their acceptance – were to be repeated in the other phases of the Conference.

These tactics were criticized as risky and dictatorial. Risky they certainly were: there was no guarantee that either side, and particularly the Front, could be brought to accept the British plan. But a reluctance to insist upon it would have carried with it not the risk but the certainty of failure. The other delegations were as determined as ever not to negotiate with each other. There was precious little common ground. The British role, therefore, could not be one of mediation, relaying one side's proposals for the other to reject. It had to be one of arbitration; and a middle line having been drawn, it could not be varied to meet the objections of either side without losing completely the confidence of the other. The most criticized aspects of British diplomacy at Lancaster House ('authoritarian', 'high-handed', 'arbitrary') were in fact the key to its success.

The Lusaka agreement had committed the British government to do no more than supervise new elections. It was clear, however, that the only arrangement which would carry conviction with the international community generally was an attempt to assume control over the Rhodesian administration while the elections were held. Yet despite its constitutional responsibility, since 1923 Britain never had exerted direct responsibility in Rhodesia. The idea of planning to do so now seemed to many foolhardy in the extreme. A British Governor, with no real force at his disposal, would be responsible for the actions of the Rhodesian forces and would have to depend on them if the Patriotic Front did not observe the cease-fire. Yet it was no use pretending that Britain still had responsibility for Rhodesia if the British government was not prepared to exercise it. Without assuming that responsibility and being ready to accept the risks that entailed, there could be no settlement. It was an understandable reluctance to grasp this nettle that had enfeebled previous efforts to achieve one.

The risks were going to be the greater since it was clear that the control really would have to be direct. The most the Muzorewa delegation initially were prepared to contemplate was the appointment of a British Governor-General, with a purely nominal role, who would have been required to act on the advice of the existing government. That, after all, was the position that had existed before UDI. Yet to command international support as well as to put Britain in a position really to direct the administration in the period before elections were held it was necessary to think not of a constitutional figurehead, but of a British Governor with full legislative and executive powers. This in turn would require the disappearance of the Rhodesian Parliament and the existing government – a fate to which Muzorewa and his Ministers were very far from being resigned.

There began another long and difficult negotiation with the Salisbury delegation. It subsequently was objected that negotiations with the Salisbury delegation were conducted privately, those with the Patriotic Front in public. But the Salisbury delegation had to be persuaded privately: it was unlikely to have been of much avail simply to call on them publicly to relinquish power. There was, meanwhile, far more private negotiation with the Front than appeared at the time.

We already had begun to discuss our ideas with those of Muzorewa's advisers in whom we had most confidence – Mundawarara, Kamusikiri, David Smith, Flower and Hawkins. His delegation were strongly opposed to Muzorewa standing aside. This, they were convinced, would be seen as weakness by the African electorate. The British role, they insisted, should be confined to supervising the elections. Most of the Bishop's African colleagues, much attached to their positions as Ministers, were fiercely opposed to standing down. The military commanders also were opposed to anything which took executive authority out of the hands of the existing government. They would have to come directly under the authority of the Governor. The moment had come at which it no longer made sense to go on dealing with General Walls through intermediaries. Peter Walls and the Police Commissioner, Peter Allum, arrived in London on 14 October to join these critical discussions.

At this time the battle with Ian Smith was still far from over. *Vis-à-vis* white opinion the crucial element now was Walls; and his opinion was likely to be no less decisive with Muzorewa. Walls prided himself on being a non-political General, and indeed had started out that way. But as Ian Smith had begun to appear to many (even of those who still voted for him) as a man who could offer them a past but no future, Walls had been catapulted into a position of prominence on the political scene. He had learned to distrust Ian Smith. By most of the whites, he was now seen as his real successor.

Walls had only recently given up the habit of parachuting with his men on operations, to say nothing of accompanying them on incursions into Mozambique. He was a charismatic figure and he enjoyed publicity. He had put his own stamp on the war, being a great advocate of an increased role for the special forces, notably the Rhodesian version of the SAS and the Selous Scouts, and of cross-border operations. He did not, however, have direct control over the army or the air force. He formed part of a collective leadership and the army, police and air force commanders never let him forget it. But he was the outstanding personality, and certainly the one most in the public view.

Walls had supported Muzorewa over the constitution and acceptance of new elections. But he and the other commanders had made clear that changes in the command or structure of the Rhodesian forces before elections took place were non-negotiable. Since Muzorewa depended on those forces for his survival, there was no doubt that this was a point on which his delegation were ready to pack their bags. We explained to Walls that our plan, unlike the Anglo-American proposals, did not entail an attempt to merge the rival armies before elections. We did not regard that as practicable. The armies would have to be merged if there were to be any prospect of peace in Zimbabwe. But the conditions of the merger would depend upon the fundamental political choice to be made by the people of Zimbabwe in free elections.

Intense efforts of persuasion continued with all the key members of the Salisbury delegation. Muzorewa, once again and not surprisingly, went through a long period of uncertainty before reaching a decision on which, he well realized, his political future and that of his country would depend. He encouraged Carrington, however, to tell his delegation clearly what steps he considered indispensable if international recognition were to be forthcoming: Carrington told them in the clearest terms that there would have to be a British Governor.

We were determined to insist on a very short transitional period with responsibility exclusively in the hands of the Governor. We believed that if we were to implement an agreement, there was a chance of success on this basis and not with any more elaborate plan. There was no practical alternative to assuming control of the existing police and administration. But Ian Smith was far from giving up. Muzorewa, he said, was like wet putty in the hands of the British. Nkomo and Mugabe were cleverer than 'our blacks'.

When Mugabe and Nkomo returned to the Conference, Carrington tabled the proposal for a British Governor with full executive and legislative authority for the pre-independence period. Nkomo and Mugabe wanted the administration to be supervised by a council consisting of four representatives of the Patriotic Front, three of the Salisbury delegation and one British representative. This would have been a recipe for deadlock, rendering any effective government impossible in the run-up to the elections.

There was not the slightest chance of the Muzorewa delegation agreeing to share power with the Front, as distinct from handing it over to Britain; and the Governor was going to face an extraordinarily difficult task in supervising the administration in the tense and dangerous period before elections. The only way to ensure that the rival political leaders were unable constantly to seek to interfere in the running of the country and thereby render his task impossible was to oblige them to commit themselves forthwith to the election campaign.

A short transitional period was no less crucial. If agreement could be reached, we would face the task of assuming direct responsibility for Rhodesia in very difficult political and military circumstances. The longer the transitional period, the greater the chances of a breakdown of the ceasefire, whether for military reasons or because one side or the other saw the political tide turning against it. Nevertheless, demands for a longer period found a good deal of sympathy among countries which would not themselves have to bear any part of the responsibility for what happened in this period. From their governments we were subjected to a deluge of advice which, for good reasons, we ignored.

We now had to face the possibility that the Patriotic Front would not agree to the transitional arrangements while Muzorewa had agreed to the constitution, new elections and a British Governor with executive authority. This was a prospect most of our friends and allies were extremely reluctant to face. But it would have been fatal to the chances of getting the Salisbury delegation to accept a British Governor's authority if the Front had been allowed to exercise a veto. It was clear that there would be applause so long as Carrington remained on the tightrope and a general rush for the exit as soon as he fell off.

As the 15 November deadline for the renewal of sanctions approached it was no less evident that any attempt to renew the Southern Rhodesia Act, even for the limited period necessary to bring the Conference to a conclusion, would place the government in difficulties with its own supporters. This, furthermore, would have been regarded as a breach of faith by the Muzorewa delegation who had agreed to the British proposals. For some time we had been considering ways of seeking to turn the parliamentary deadline to advantage in the negotiations.

Instead, therefore, of simply letting sanctions – or most

of them – lapse, we proceeded to introduce in Parliament an enabling Bill designed to increase the momentum towards a settlement by giving the government all the powers it needed to make provision for the independence constitution, new elections and a return to legality – thereby demonstrating to both sides that we meant business and intended to proceed with a settlement.

My dealings with her over the Bill were my first direct experience of Margaret Thatcher who, reminding me that she was a lawyer, insisted on going through every clause of it, before agreeing that it should be done. Muzorewa and his delegation were told that all sanctions would be removed on the day the Governor arrived in Salisbury, and his authority was accepted – and not before.

By this stage even Ian Smith was saying that he accepted the British plan. 'The Rhodesian Front have come to the end of the road in the London talks.' There was nothing more to be gained by holding out. On his return to Salisbury on 11 November, he warned the white community to prepare for the arrival of Nkomo and Mugabe. The British, he said, were determined to have them in.

The Front continued to argue that it would take two months to bring a cease-fire into effect and that free elections could not be held under the existing police. Carrington replied that the Police Commissioner would be answerable to the Governor and the Rhodesian police would be monitored by British police advisers. Mugabe raised reasonable questions about the impartiality and continuance in office of the Chief Justice, Hector Macdonald, who had delivered some highly political sentences and condemned a number of guerrillas to death. Macdonald, who was in London, agreed that Carrington might state that, in the event of a Patriotic Front victory, he would not wish to continue to serve on the High Court.

President Kaunda was invited to London as the moment of decision approached. Zambia had suffered greatly for its 15 years of support for Nkomo and his followers. The Rhodesians were reaching ever deeper into Zambia in their raids on ZIPRA targets. The country was in increasingly desperate economic straits. The rail-line to Tanzania was almost inoperative, as was the Benguela railway through

Angola. As the Kazangula ferry to Botswana also had been destroyed by the Rhodesians, the only reliable outlet for Zambian exports was via Rhodesia Railways, though the two countries virtually were in a state of war.

Kenneth Kaunda had more than almost anyone to gain from the success of the negotiations. It remained unclear, however, how decisively he would be prepared to exert his influence. His personal commitment to the independence struggle was very strong; and to it he had often been prepared to sacrifice Zambian interests. In the margins of the Lancaster House Conference his personal representative, Mark Chona, seemed on occasions to be defending positions already abandoned by Nkomo.

Mrs Thatcher and Carrington sought to impress on Kaunda that this was the moment for decisions, if ever there was one. There was a real danger of the Muzorewa delegation leaving the Conference if the Patriotic Front continued to filibuster. An agreement was attainable on the basis Carrington had proposed, but not otherwise. In contrast to other attempts to achieve a settlement, the British government was in a position to put these plans into effect. Nkomo was showing interest in an agreement: it would be a tragedy if the chance were lost. Carrington proceeded also to lift the veil on the British proposals for the cease-fire, including the establishment of a cease-fire commission with equal representation for the Patriotic Front and the Rhodesian commanders, a monitoring force and assurances that provision would be made for the Patriotic Front forces.

Kaunda reacted positively. Nkomo realized that a decision could no longer be delayed. On 14 November, in a critical phase of the Conference, Carrington told the Patriotic Front leaders that if it were not possible to reach agreement, he would have to report the position to his Cabinet colleagues at 10.30 a.m. the next day and ask them to decide their future course of action.

On the following morning it was clear that Nkomo was prepared to agree. Mugabe was more reluctant. Both were aware by this time that the enabling Bill had passed both Houses of Parliament and that, if they refused, it was open to the British government to try to proceed with the internal parties. After a break during which the Patriotic Front leaders conferred together, a plenary session was held at 10 a.m. Mugabe stated that with an addition to the British paper according some recognition to the Patriotic Front forces, they could accept the pre-independence proposals, subject to a successful outcome of the negotiations on the cease-fire. Another exercise in brinkmanship had worked.

6 Negotiation

Each successive phase of the Conference was more difficult than the last. The problems which, from the outset, had appeared certain to cause most difficulty were the military arrangements for the cease-fire and the separation of the forces. Hence the strategy of tackling these only after agreement on the political issues had created momentum, and some expectation of success.

It was necessary first to persuade the Rhodesian commanders: without their agreement, there would be no settlement to implement. Muzorewa was in no position to overrule them. Peter Walls had said repeatedly that there was no military solution to the war. Following the April elections, he believed that Muzorewa had more political support than the Patriotic Front; and he was convinced of the need for a settlement at any rate with Britain if he was to have any chance of turning the military tide. The Rhodesian commanders were determined, however, that they should not be placed at a military disadvantage, with their forces confined to barracks while the guerrillas continued to operate freely in the tribal trust lands; and they were haunted by the dangers of relinquishing control. Nor were they prepared to accept a UN or Commonwealth peace-keeping force.

Walls was told that the British government did not envisage UN involvement, though there would be a need for a monitoring force. There would also be a cease-fire commission with equal Patriotic Front participation. The Rhodesian forces would not be placed at a military disadvantage. Our concept was based on reciprocal disengagement. If Patriotic Front forces remained active after the cease-fire, the Rhodesian forces would have to be authorized to assist the police in dealing with them.

The Rhodesian commanders argued that any disengagement which gave the Front's forces status within Rhodesia before the elections would be damaging to Muzorewa and virtually impossible to control militarily. They did not believe that there would be a fully effective cease-fire and in this they were quite right. We also thought it sensible to plan on the basis of a less than fully effective cease-fire. The difficulties of devising an effective plan were great. The opposing forces were inextricably entangled throughout Rhodesia. The Rhodesians would not agree to a cease-fire *sur place*. This in any case would have been certain to break down and would have rendered impossible any effective monitoring arrangement. The Rhodesian conception was either that the Patriotic Front forces should withdraw to their bases in Zambia and Mozambique; or that there should be no cease-fire until *after* the elections!

No previous British government had contemplated sending British forces to Rhodesia; and there were obvious risks in doing so. Mrs Thatcher had said in Lusaka that she did not envisage sending British troops. Yet it was clear that no cease-fire could be maintained without a monitoring force. After much persuasion, Walls was brought to agree to a force under British auspices with participation from the few Commonwealth countries not formally committed to support the Front (Australia, New Zealand, Fiji and Kenya). We concluded that a readiness to take responsibility for the monitoring force and to make the major contribution to it was crucial to the chances of success.

It was clear that the demarcation of zones between the two sides would have been impossible to negotiate. The Patriotic Front forces would have to assemble and be identified if their activities were to be monitored and their security guaranteed. General Walls was also demanding the monitoring of Patriotic Front bases *outside* Rhodesia.

Our problems were increased by the Rhodesian refusal to engage in direct negotiations with the Patriotic Front commanders. Tongogara insisted that he should deal with Walls. I needed no convincing of this. But just as Mugabe and Nkomo had refused to negotiate with Muzorewa on the grounds that he was a puppet, so now Muzorewa would not authorize, and nor would Walls agree to, direct talks with the Patriotic Front commanders. We had no option, therefore, but to undertake ourselves the negotiations with both sides.

This meant that every morning in the Foreign Office, with our experts from the Ministry of Defence, I held meetings with the Rhodesian commanders, led by Peter Walls. Each afternoon, there was a meeting with the Patriotic Front commanders – Dabengwa of ZIPRA and Tongogara of ZANLA. These talks got off to a sticky start, with Dabengwa still under instructions to talk to no one but Walls. But Tongogara established a good relationship with General Farndale, Director of Military Operations in the Ministry of Defence, and the rest of the British team. His attitude was much more positive. He started by insisting on a large Commonwealth or UN force to enforce the cease-fire, by which he meant to neutralize the Rhodesian forces. It was explained to him that it could not be the task of a British or Commonwealth force to fight the Rhodesian army – or the Patriotic Front. The responsibility for keeping the peace must lie with the commanders on both sides. The monitoring force would be there to help them maintain the cease-fire and to ensure the safety of the Patriotic Front forces as they assembled. It was a concept Tongogara in the end accepted.

The Rhodesians insisted that the assembly process must be completed within seven days. The period in which they broke off contact with the guerrillas and moved back towards their bases, relinquishing control over much of the countryside, was bound to be one of extreme tension, and in which they saw great dangers, including risks to Muzorewa's supporters and the white community. The guerrilla commanders, no less naturally, regarded the whole idea of assembling their forces as extremely dangerous. Given the capabilities of the Rhodesian air force and fire forces, the safety of the guerrillas lay in their mobility and ability to disappear among the rural population. It was asking a great deal of the guerrilla armies to emerge from the countryside and assemble in positions where they would be vulnerable to attack.

Nkomo and Mugabe continued to insist that it would take two months for their forces to assemble and a cease-fire to be brought into effect. But a prolonged assembly process, with large groups of guerrillas moving openly about the country with their arms, was liable to lead not to consolidation of the cease-fire, but to a rapid resumption of the war. Since the reason given for this demand was the supposed difficulty of getting orders through to the guerrillas in the bush, I reminded Tongogara of the case of Mrs Mulligan, a Rhodesian farmer's wife kidnapped by ZANLA and, since she could not walk that far, pushed by them in a wheelbarrow much of the 200 kilometres to the Mozambique border! Tongogara cheerfully acknowledged that he could get orders to all his forces inside Rhodesia within three or four days. The ZANLA command structure was to prove far more effective than the Rhodesians ever imagined, though fringe elements of ZANLA were outside anyone's effective control.

While conversations with the Patriotic Front commanders, or at any rate with Tongogara, had taken this more promising turn, the prospects of success in the Conference were nearly destroyed by massive Rhodesian raids into Zambia. Nkomo was trying to get as many men as possible across the border in anticipation either of a settlement or of the need to try to intensify the war if there seemed a disposition to proceed without him. On 5 November the Rhodesians tightened their economic stranglehold by cutting off maize supplies to Zambia.

The attacks on Zambia a fortnight later were authorized by the military commanders in Salisbury without, so Walls claimed, reference to him in London. They did impede ZIPRA movement towards the Rhodesian border. But they clearly were designed also to inflict maximum damage on the Zambian infrastructure. Kaunda professed to be convinced that the attacks had been authorized by Britain. There were demonstrations outside the British offices in Lusaka and the High Commissioner had to be withdrawn. The Rhodesians offered not to conduct further cross-border operations in return for the cessation of cross-border movement by the Front. Nkomo and Mugabe refused. The Rhodesians were warned of the consequences of any further exploits of this kind. It proved possible just in time to prevent them blowing up the Tete suspension bridge in Mozambique.

The Mozambique government and Tongogara were continuing to show keen interest in the British cease-fire proposals. Throughout the Conference, President Machel's representative in London (Fernando Honwana) had made clear his interest in helping to achieve a settlement, if one was obtainable on terms fair to ZANU. Honwana had his President's confidence. Conscious of the enormous benefits an agreement would bring to Mozambique, among the representatives of the African states he played by far the most important role in the negotiations. A few years later he was tragically killed in the same plane-crash as Samora Machel. Tongogara remained concerned about the security of his forces once they assembled. Mugabe and Nkomo continued to demand that the Rhodesian forces must be confined to barracks. Carrington assured them that their forces would retain their arms and would remain under the authority of their own commanders. The Rhodesian forces would be monitored. Since Mugabe was convinced that if the Front won there would be a coup, he was assured that the monitoring force would stay in Rhodesia until the independence government was formed.

The Front were also concerned about South African involvement and intentions. There were known to be several hundred South African personnel serving with the Rhodesian forces. Although it was less well-known at the time, there also were several hundred FRELIMO soldiers from Mozambique operating with ZANLA in the eastern provinces. Walls was told that there must be no South African military units on Rhodesian territory during the transition.

With the military temperature rising rapidly in and around Rhodesia it was clear that unless action was taken to bring the negotiations to a rapid conclusion, all the gains that had been made were likely very soon to be lost. We concluded that if the Front could be brought to accept the cease-fire proposals, a plan must be devised to deal with the danger of indefinitely prolonged discussion of the arrangements for their implementation. The only way to get through what looked to be a fast-narrowing gap was to accelerate.

To step up the pressure on the parties to agree, on 3 December the British government made the Order in Council providing for the appointment of a Governor with full executive and legislative authority. Carrington gave a press conference to say that Britain was beginning to take the legislative action to put the settlement into effect, but in such a way as to leave it open for the Front to participate.

The Rhodesians by this time had been pushed into proposing a number of places at which the Patriotic Front forces might assemble within the country. These were all in peripheral areas where guerrilla activity had been intense and which were in close proximity to the frontiers. These locations did not have much appeal to the Front's political leaders. They did correspond, however, to Tongogara's concern that his forces should not be encircled by the Rhodesians, and should have their backs to the Mozambique border. The Rhodesians subsequently were pressed into agreeing to two or three assembly places in more central areas. One of these, Assembly point Foxtrot in the Sabi tribal trust land, into which ZANU packed 6000 men, was to prove a headache throughout the transition. Nkomo remained concerned, on political grounds, about the absence of an assembly point for his forces in the Midlands. Following the selection of 15 assembly places, associated rendezvous points were chosen to enable the guerrillas to assemble under the auspices of the monitoring force and be taken to the assembly camps.

The preparations for the return to legality had already been set in hand. From the end of November a British military team under Brigadier Adam Gurdon, who had done much to help devise these plans, was engaged in reconnoitring the assembly places and making practical preparations.

In meetings with the Patriotic Front, the argument continued over the cease-fire arrangements. Sir Antony Duff made clear in the Conference that if Patriotic Front forces remained in the field with their arms, elements of the Rhodesian forces would be deployed against them. The Rhodesians insisted that the period of disengagement when the Rhodesian forces would break off contact with the guerrillas and stand back from the assembly places and the routes towards them could not be prolonged for more than a week. As we would be responsible for the country at the time, we were no less anxious as to what might happen in this, the most dangerous phase of the cease-fire. A short assembly period was crucial to the chances of keeping the military situation under control, but would be tolerable only on the basis, which was agreed, that the cease-fire date must be preceded by an adequate period of preparation to allow the guerrilla commanders as well as the Rhodesians to get their orders through to their forces in the field.

7 Agreement

I was an unashamed advocate of Christopher Soames as the future Governor of Rhodesia, if we did manage to get close to an agreement. I had served with him in Paris where he was, arguably, the most effective Ambassador we had sent there since the war. A great friend of Carrington, he was a senior member of the Cabinet and leader of the House of Lords. We were going to need someone who would make up in force of personality what he lacked in real power.

I was with Carrington in his office when he telephoned Soames to break to him the news that the Prime Minister wanted him to go to Rhodesia. The surprise at the other end of the line was palpable but Soames, characteristically, barely hesitated before agreeing to take on this near-impossible task. When, afterwards, he asked me why I had lobbied so hard on his behalf, I told him that I knew that we were going to have a difficult time in Rhodesia, but that with him as Governor, at least we would never be down to our last bottle of champagne.

By this stage it was clear that unless we moved quickly the chance of a settlement would be lost as a result of a military crisis or the withdrawal of Muzorewa's delegation.

On 7 December Ian Gilmour announced in Parliament Soames' appointment as Governor of Rhodesia and that he would arrive in Salisbury in the following week. The Rhodesian Parliament would be dissolved. The presence of a British authority was essential to put a settlement into effect.

There still was no certainty that the Patriotic Front would participate. They were intensifying their efforts to infiltrate more of their forces into Rhodesia. ZIPRA were trying to push large units across the Rhodesia/Zambia border. The Rhodesians were getting ready to launch a new series of pre-emptive attacks. Maize supplies to Zambia were still cut off. Unless agreement on a cease-fire was reached within a few days, it was unlikely to be reached at all.

We now faced the expected difficulty of bringing the Conference to a conclusion. Unless the Patriotic Front were aware that the establishment of British authority and the lifting of sanctions were actually under way, they would have no incentive to end the negotiation because they believed it in their political and military interests to prolong it. If, however, they were given a strong enough push, it looked as if it should be possible to bring them in. They had only been pushed over previous hurdles by the threat of proceeding without them. Now they were being asked to take the final decision which committed them to the whole agreement. On this occasion they were only likely to be persuaded to jump by the sight of the bus actually leaving the station.

On 11 December Carrington made a final presentation of the cease-fire proposals. Maps were distributed with details of the Patriotic Front assembly places and the arrangements for monitoring the Rhodesian forces. The final decision to send Soames to Salisbury was not taken until that morning. This was the biggest gamble of the whole Conference. Manifestly there were very big risks involved. On the basis of our contacts with key members of their delegations and because there would be strong pressure on them to do so, there seemed a good prospect that the Front could be brought to accept the final cease-fire proposals. A delay in sending the Governor, however, would have removed all pressure on them to agree, as well as causing a crisis with the Rhodesian delegation, who would have been instructed to return to Salisbury and see whether parliamentary pressures in Britain forced the lifting of the remaining sanctions, while both sides intensified the war. To put an end to these uncertainties, Carrington announced in Parliament that evening the departure of Soames for Rhodesia.

The decision to cross this Rubicon, although essential to bring the Conference to a close, caused much heart-searching on the part of other Western countries, who remained reluctant to be confronted with anything approaching a choice between Britain and the Front. In New York, Sir Anthony Parsons informed the UN Security Council that with the arrival of a British Governor and the acceptance of his authority, lawful government had been restored in Rhodesia. The sanctions applied by Britain were being lifted forthwith.

The chances of finally pushing the Front into a settlement, however, still depended on the extent of the support we received. Within the US Administration, opinions were divided. Some US officials saw themselves as leading a campaign to 'save the British from themselves'. The US Embassy in London had more confidence in our negotiating tactics, which they regarded as brutal, certainly, but in a respectable cause. On 16 December President Carter approved the lifting of sanctions, a move which helped to bring home to the Front the consequences of further delay.

En route to Rhodesia, Soames telephoned me from his aircraft to urge that a further effort should be made with Mugabe and Nkomo. Nkomo by this stage was ready to agree provided he secured an additional assembly place for his forces. But Mugabe still sounded intransigent. On 13 December, Muzorewa's delegation formally accepted the detailed proposals for the cease-fire.

Nkomo said that Soames would now be responsible for the conduct of the war. Ian Gilmour told Mugabe and Nkomo that if the Front accepted the agreement, we were bound to ensure that it was implemented honourably. Carrington said that it was not possible to grant the Front bases in areas where they had never been able to establish them by military means. The purpose of the cease-fire agreement was not to grant one side or the other political advantages, but to enable elections to be held.

Robert Mugabe continued to object that if his forces concentrated they would be at a disadvantage if – as he clearly expected – they had to start fighting again. These concerns were understandable. It was no small matter to ask a guerrilla army, whose safety lay in its dispersal, to emerge from the bush and assemble in camps where they would be vulnerable to attack by the Rhodesian forces. We pointed out that if they were attacked our forces, monitoring the camps, would be most at risk of all. But he was not yet convinced.

The final session of the Conference was held on the morning of Saturday 15 December. It resulted in no agreement. While Nkomo looked unhappy, Mugabe attacked the British proposals. The Front, he said, did not accept the cease-fire and were not bound by any of the agreements reached at the Conference. Mundawarara initialled the conference documents on behalf of Muzorewa and left forthwith for Rhodesia.

The Conference formally thus ended in failure. Throughout the weekend, however, efforts were made to persuade the Patriotic Front leaders to think again. It was clear that Nkomo still wanted an agreement; but Mugabe was preparing to leave for New York to address the United Nations. Soames in Salisbury was asked to impress on the Rhodesian commanders that it was in Rhodesia's interests and crucial to the prospects of international acceptance that a final effort should be made to bring in the Front, by the offer of an additional assemby place. General Walls regarded this as going back on agreements already entered into. On the Sunday morning, nevertheless, the Patriotic Front leaders, still in London, were told that they would receive an additional assembly place.

This was what Nkomo required in order to give his agreement. He was convinced that, otherwise, he would indeed miss the bus. *Vis-à-vis* ZANU, however, the situation was more difficult. By far the most effective intervention came from President Machel. We had assured his representative, Fernando Honwana, that if ZANU participated, their forces would be looked after and they would get a fair chance to win the elections. Honwana delivered to ZANU a message from Samora Machel urging them to sign and warning that if they did not, they could no longer count on Mozambican support. Nyerere had been helpful in assuring Machel that the British did not know how to rig an election! Tongogara, after hesitating about the military arrangements, also came down in favour of agreement. On the Sunday evening Mugabe telephoned Charles Powell to say that ZANU also would agree.

For ZANU, Tongogara signed in my office the map giving the co-ordinates of all the assembly places for his forces. He told me that he was convinced it was the right thing to do, but the agreement carried enormous risks for him and his men.

I pointed out, once again, that our troops would be at even greater risk if ZANLA were attacked in the assembly places. If the war continued, ZANLA might well win, but the victory would not be easy. In the event of a breakdown, the South Africans were likely to intervene not just to help the whites get out, but also to inflict as much damage as possible on the guerrilla forces. The economy and infra-

structure would be destroyed. ZANU would inherit a country as devastated as Mozambique. All this Tongogara acknowledged. On leaving, he declared his determination to see
the cease-fire implemented and belief that this could be done
in the allotted time-scale.

At 6 p.m. on Monday 17 December Nkomo and Mugabe
called on Ian Gilmour – in Carrington's absence with Mrs
Thatcher in Washington – to initial the agreement. Against
what had seemed at the outset impossible odds, the Conference had ended in agreement that the rival armies should
lay down their arms, accept a return to colonial rule and
permit a British Governor to arrange for them to settle their
differences in elections. *Ex Africa semper aliquid novo.*

The successful completion of what had appeared an almost impossible negotiation was attributable to a number
of factors. The neighbouring countries were looking for an
escape from the war; the Lusaka agreement offered them
one. The Rhodesians knew that they could no longer carry
on without an agreement with Britain at least. Ian Smith
was not able to bring his negative influence so directly to
bear. Nkomo was conscious that this was his last chance,
but afraid of being accused of splitting the Patriotic Front.
Despite subsequent difficulties with him, Peter Walls' influence in favour of a settlement was crucial. The South Africans were persuaded to acquiesce. We found an unexpected
ally in Samora Machel, whose intervention was decisive at
the end.

The timing was right. This would not, however, have been
of much avail without the determination with which, this
time, the British government tackled the problem and the
manner in which Carrington conducted the negotiations. It
was the ambition of everyone involved in them finally to
discharge Britain's responsibility to bring Rhodesia to legal
independence and to do so in a fashion which would en-
hance our reputation and not diminish it. The government
took the difficult and courageous decisions to send Soames
to Rhodesia in advance of final agreement in the Conference and to send several hundred British troops to monitor
a precarious cease-fire. Without a willingness to take those
decisions and face the risks they involved, a settlement would
not have been achieved.

There remained the fundamental difficulty that the Rhodesians who, by the end of the Conference, were more or less resigned to the inclusion of Nkomo, were never really reconciled to the participation of ZANU. The Lancaster House Conference had ended in a success beyond reasonable expectations. It was clear to all of us that if the difficulties of negotiating the agreement had been great, they were going to be a lot less formidable than the task of implementing it.

8 A British Governor

Christopher Soames set off for Salisbury with understandable misgivings. Far from being over, the war had developed a new intensity as ZIPRA and ZANLA tried to get the bulk of their forces in Zambia and Mozambique into Rhodesia and the Rhodesians responded with ferocious cross-border raids. In the absence of agreement with the Front, no African country would grant clearance for Soames' aircraft which, therefore, had to take him to Rhodesia via the Azores and Ascension Island.

Soames saw great dangers in assuming, in effect, responsibility for the actions of the Rhodesian forces, who would now nominally be under his control, in the midst of a war. He would have preferred agreement with the Front to be reached and a cease-fire concluded before he assumed control. But the chances of bringing the negotiation to a conclusion depended on Britain proceeding forthwith to assume direct responsibility, putting itself into a position to make the necessary preparations on the ground for a cease-fire and exerting decisive pressure on the Front to take the plunge. When Soames left London, there still was no certainty that they would do so. The reaction from ZANU was violent, with their spokesman stating that, in the absence of a cease-fire, the Governor would be a party to the war and a military target. His wife, Mary, characteristically, made clear that, come what may, she was going too.

Soames, accompanied by the Deputy Governor, Antony Duff, the Election Commissioner, Sir John Boynton, and the Commander of the Commonwealth Monitoring Force, Major-General Acland, arrived at Salisbury airport on the afternoon of 12 December. As Ian Smith considered further resistance to be useless, the Salisbury Parliament had voted unanimously at midnight on the previous day for its own dissolution. Muzorewa, as he ceased to be Prime Minister, called on the population to support Soames in the 'unenviable task' of administering the country until elections took place. At the arrival ceremony, in a moment of some emotion, the police band played 'God Save The Queen'. This had required some days of practice, the anthem having been banished with the proclamation by the Rhodesian Front of Rhodesia as a Republic in 1969. Outside Government House, a small group of loyalists waved flags as Soames arrived. They had waited for this moment a long time. Many of them had struggled for 15 years against the Smith regime, winning few votes, incurring in the small society of white Rhodesia much obloquy and never able to exert much influence, but keeping the flag of decency flying.

At Government House, the Union Jack was raised. Among those there to greet Soames was Sir Humphrey Gibbs, Governor at the time of UDI. In a broadcast that evening Soames said that his task was to hold the government of the country in trust until independence. International recognition would depend on the elections, in which all parties must be given the chance to participate. 'For a war-weary country the prize is great.' Ian Smith replied that Rhodesia was going through the darkest period of its history, having been compelled for the first time to hand over control to outsiders.

Within Rhodesia as outside, it was regarded as far from clear that Soames' mission had any chance of success. In Britain some of the newspapers, recalling what had happened in Saigon, wondered if he might not have to make his exit in a helicopter from the grounds of Government House. Cartoonists delighted in depicting Soames, in knee-length shorts, stepping into a river full of crocodiles. The election results, it was suggested, might best be announced by megaphone from an aircraft as he was leaving.

Rhodesian attacks on Zambia and Mozambique ended with Soames' arrival. But within the country the war continued. Combined Operations Headquarters continued to report the 'normal' toll of daily casualties. Pending agreement on a cease-fire, ZANU and ZAPU remained banned. Soames' first real act of authority was to order the resumption of rail shipments of maize to Zambia. General Acland and his staff pressed on with the preparations for a cease-fire which might still not take place. At a press conference, Acland declared that there were about a thousand South African troops in Rhodesia. This was no more than confirmation of what everyone knew already to be the case. But, the press and the

Front wanted to know, what was Soames going to do about it?

The South African troop presence was a matter which, for all its importance, was going to have to be dealt with later. The final session of the Lancaster House Conference had ended on 15 December without agreement. The ZANU spokesman, Eddison Zvobgo, said that the war would continue and 'the implications are horrendous'.

Even if a cease-fire was agreed, General Acland found, on the part of the Rhodesian military, astonishment that the monitoring force should be prepared to take on a task so fraught with danger in the rendezvous and assembly points, all of them in areas of intense guerrilla activity. These attitudes of course were coloured by the years of war against the Patriotic Front. The Rhodesians doubted the authority of the guerrilla commanders over many of their men and their ability to subject them to any kind of discipline. Having negotiated directly with them, we had more confidence in their command structure. But it was clear that the monitoring force would be on a knife-edge from cease-fire day, when the monitoring teams would be left on their own in widely dispersed areas awaiting the arrival of the Patriotic Front forces, until the assembly process was completed.

These problems still lay ahead. To have a chance of getting a cease-fire at all, it was necessary to offer the Front an additional assembly place, beyond what had been agreed by the Muzorewa delegation at Lancaster House. We were not prepared to let the negotiations break down on an issue of this kind without having made a final and determined effort to succeed. The Americans were expected to lift sanctions within 48 hours. They would also require to be satisfied that a final effort had been made with the Patriotic Front. General Walls regarded this as an unpleasant foretaste of things to come. With Nkomo now prepared to sign, however, and Mugabe under pressure from President Machel to do so, we were determined to proceed.

The early days of Soames' administration were dominated by this crisis with the Rhodesian military. They would have preferred to hold the Front at bay while another election was held, confined to the internal parties. Belatedly, they had begun to see some advantage in an attempt to include Nkomo. This appealed as offering the prospect of enabling them to deal with ZANLA in what would then have become a one-front war. Now, thanks to the intervention of Machel, they found themselves with the Front as a whole in the agreement. The Rhodesian commanders were never reconciled to the participation of ZANU in the settlement. They did not believe that ZANU would comply with the cease-fire, or campaign peacefully. They had counted on the Shona votes going to Muzorewa. Muzorewa was advised by Walls and his colleagues not to sign the agreement unless he got categorical assurances that any party violating the cease-fire and engaging in widespread intimidation would be disqualified from the elections.

We pressed ahead with the practical preparations for the cease-fire. The US Air Force were asked to airlift to Rhodesia tents for 20 000 men to accommodate the Patriotic Front forces. Walls and his colleagues were told that we did not intend to let any party win by cheating. We were not, however, prepared to enter into any categorical undertakings as to what action Soames might take. That would depend on how determined an effort was made by the Front to assemble their forces, the conduct of whatever forces failed to assemble and the observance of the cease-fire. Nkomo, moving quickly to start mending his fences with the white community, gave an interview to the *Rhodesia Herald* declaring his intention to work for reconciliation. The *Herald* applauded the conclusion of the Conference as one of the most significant diplomatic coups Britain was ever likely to achieve; but, it added, luck as well as skill would be needed to see the country through to the elections.

On his return to London for the signature ceremony, Muzorewa sought reassurance from Carrington. The ceremony took place at Lancaster House on 21 December. In his speech, Carrington stated that *no party could expect to participate in the elections if it continued the war and systematically broke the cease-fire.* The agreement, he added, gave the people of Rhodesia new hope for the future.

Nkomo was still proceeding on the assumption that the Front would fight the elections together. He was aware of his lack of support outside Matabeleland, though he refused to believe that it had evaporated altogether. No doubt he also hoped that in such an alliance, as the 'senior' political leader, he might be called upon to form the first government of independent Zimbabwe, with Mugabe as his deputy. ZANU had no intention of allowing this to happen. They considered that they had done most of the fighting and had the support of the bulk of the population.

Throughout the Conference, despite frequent differences between the parties, it had never looked likely that Nkomo would break with ZANU. Mugabe was made of steelier stuff. Despite pressure from the Commonwealth African presidents on the Front to stay united, he proceeded to liquidate the alliance with ZAPU. On 30 December, the day before the parties were required to register, Enos Nkala, leader of the internal wing of ZANU, announced that the party would fight the elections alone. In the event of ZANU forming the next government, Nkomo would be offered the honorific position of President.

On 21 December, the day of the signature of the Lancaster House Agreement, Soames lifted the bans on ZAPU and ZANU and granted a general amnesty. The first transport aircraft carrying British troops and equipment began to arrive in Salisbury. Rhodesian special forces still operating in Zambia, disconcerted by the noise of this armada, withdrew across the Zambesi. Nkomo made a broadcast giving instructions for his forces to cease fire at the appointed time – midnight on 28 December – and report to the assembly places.

The Conference over, I left to join Soames in Rhodesia. On Boxing Day, the first group of guerrilla commanders arrived at Salisbury airport. The ZIPRA team, led by Lookout Masuku, flew in from Lusaka in the morning; the ZANLA contingent, led by Rex Nhongo, from Maputo in the afternoon.

These were tense moments as the guerrilla leaders came face to face with officers of the Rhodesian police, many of whom had been engaged no less actively than the army in the war. The police behaved correctly, and so did the guerrilla commanders. The Rhodesian army included in the welcoming party two armoured cars. These were ordered off the tarmac by Major Andrew Parker-Bowles of the monitoring force. The guerrilla leaders were greeted by a large and turbulent crowd; in camouflage uniforms, newly issued for the occasion, they were taken by bus to their headquarters close to the university campus. Traffic came to an astonished standstill on the tranquil suburban roads as these convoys skirted the town.

Nkomo by now had broadcast a series of statements to his forces about the cease-fire. But considerable uncertainty still surrounded ZANU's intentions. The tone of Mugabe's pronouncements remained extremely militant. On Christmas Eve he said that two weeks to implement a cease-fire was ridiculous. It would take more like two months. South African forces were still in Rhodesia. 'We need lots of arms: the war is not yet over.' He would return to Rhodesia once the cease-fire was effective. Mugabe's suspicions as to what might await him when he did return had been deepened by an attack on the house of his sister in Salisbury on 22 December in which two of his nephews were slightly injured – an attack which appeared to be the work of youth elements of Muzorewa's party.

On 27 December, Mugabe told the British Ambassador in Maputo that Tongogara had been killed in a road accident north of Maputo in the early hours of Boxing Day. He was to have driven through the night to his headquarters near Chimoio with instructions for the cease-fire. Tungamirai and two others accompanying Tongogara survived the crash. Mugabe broadcast his cease-fire message over Radio Maputo, adding that British imperialism would be trying to run in the elections 'under cover of the puppet Muzorewa'.

The news of Tongogara's death was a serious blow. We had established a good rapport with him at Lancaster House. He had shown himself more committed than others to a settlement, once convinced that one was attainable on terms that would offer ZANU a fair chance of winning the elections. His worries about the security of his forces once they assembled had been overcome by the siting of most of the ZANLA camps close to the Mozambique border in territory all of which was ZANLA-controlled at night anyway; and by his realization that the monitoring force in the assembly places would be at equal risk in the event of any Rhodesian attack. Throughout the negotiations on the cease-fire conducted in the margins of the Conference, Tongogara had insisted that many of these problems could be sorted out direct between him and Walls, for whose professional competence and that of the Rhodesian forces generally he had a healthy respect. Although direct talks had proved impossible to organize in London, we had hoped that, once in Rhodesia, Walls and Tongogara could be brought together to discuss the future integration of the forces. We had counted heavily also on Tongogara's authority to help in securing compliance with the cease-fire and in defusing the military confrontations likely to take place in the period of the assembly of the guerrilla forces.

Tongogara's death at this crucial moment gave rise to all sorts of suspicions – the more so as he was known to have met Nkomo before leaving London and had been in favour of the Front fighting the elections together. There was no evidence, however, that his death was anything other than an accident. The Mozambican government held their own enquiry. At Mugabe's request, we arranged for Rhodesian help in having Tongogara's body embalmed and taken to his birthplace near Selukwe for burial. Mugabe, meanwhile, gave a further interview in Maputo, demanding to know what would happen to the South African troops still in Rhodesia before ZANLA transferred its men to the assembly places.

9 The Cease-fire

In the short time they had been in Rhodesia, the monitoring force had accomplished prodigies of improvisation. A reconnaissance party had been in the country since 22 November. On 12 December General Acland and his senior staff had arrived with Soames. They had just ten days to prepare for the arrival of the bulk of the force, immediately the Lancaster House agreement was signed. As the British officers made contact with the Rhodesian military in the regions, they found it to be universally assumed that the small and isolated monitoring force teams would be attacked on their first night in the field. The force consisted of 850 British troops, mainly officers and NCOs, 159 Australians, 75 New Zealanders, 51 Kenyans and 24 Fijians. Of the 14 assembly places eventually established and consolidated, five were manned principally by the British, four by the Australians, three by the New Zealanders and one each by the Kenyans and Fijians. Monitoring teams were attached also to the Rhodesian military headquarters in the regions and forces down to company level; and to the Patriotic Front headquarters in Salisbury.

From 22 December US Air Force Galaxies and RAF transport aircraft brought in the full complement of men and vast quantities of stores and equipment. The Rhodesians provided a tented transit camp, but the monitoring force contingents spent less than a week in it before deployment to the most remote and dangerous part of the country.

Their instructions were to show 'an overt and friendly presence so that Patriotic Front personnel will be reassured enough to come forward to report to your rendez-vous point'. The first contact, they were told, was likely to be made by *mujibas*, young and generally unarmed supporters of the Front. If satisfied that this was not a trap, they would report back to their leaders. One or two armed guerrillas might then be sent in to test the system. They should be permitted to go back into the bush to report. Eventually a squad would arrive with an identifiable leader. It would be for the Patriotic Front liaison officer with each group to deal with him. The monitoring teams were only to accept armed men. Unarmed men were to be turned away. Women were to be accepted only if they were armed. On no account was any attempt to be made to disarm any of the guerrillas. Those who reported were to be offered food, cigarettes and medical help and supplied with blankets and clothing. At night too, the presence must be overt and the site illuminated. If the monitoring teams came under attack, they were instructed to stay put. In that event, General Acland would have been obliged to call on the Rhodesian forces to help disengage them. The Rhodesians fully expected to have to do this, sooner rather than later.

On 27 and 28 December these small teams began to move out into the countryside, and those of Soames' advisers who had helped to negotiate the agreement at Lancaster House passed through some of the worst hours of their lives. It required an enormous leap of faith to believe that this immensely difficult operation could be accomplished without casualties or some major clash as one or more of the guerrilla groups got out of control. Already three members of the RAF had been killed in a helicopter crash. An RAF Hercules reconnoitring an assembly place near the Mozambique border had been fired on, the bullet making a neat hole in the middle of the large white cross on the wing of the monitoring force plane.

The monitoring force contingents were escorted during 28 December to many of the rendezvous points by mine-clearing vehicles of the Rhodesian police. The RAF Hercules flew innumerable sorties in appalling weather. As a result of torrential rain, some of the dirt tracks were well-nigh impassable. Nevertheless by cease-fire time, midnight on 28 December, 35 of the 39 teams had reached the rendezvous points. The remaining four were in a position to do so by first light on the following day.

Having put up their flags, they waited. Everything depended on the courage, self-control and judgement of the young officers and NCOs. One serious error, any major clash, would have prejudiced the position of the force as a whole. Faced with the superior firepower of the Rhodesian forces, safety for the guerrillas had lain in their dispersal. Required now to assemble, they did so in conditions of extreme tension, conscious of their vulnerability and suspecting a trap, inclined at first to see the Commonwealth troops in much the same light as the Rhodesian forces. Each team had to overcome a series of tense and difficult situations. It was their gallantry which prevented casualties occurring and rescued Rhodesia from the war. The Hercules and helicopter crews showed similar courage in rushing supplies to where they were needed, landing on small and difficult airstrips, which had only just been cleared of mines.

In the course of the first day of the cease-fire, about 500 guerrillas moved into the rendezvous points with their arms. Some, having made contact with the monitoring teams, went back into the bush to consult with their commanders. As the Rhodesian forces pulled back from the border, there appeared the first signs of cross-border movement on a major scale by ZANLA from Mozambique. ZANLA groups were organizing victory marches through villages on the eastern border. The second day showed a similar pattern, with ZANLA groups crossing the border, not moving directly to the assembly places and staging marches to 'politicize' the local population. Retaliation by the Rhodesian forces against a large ZANLA contingent which had crossed the border north of Umtali was narrowly avoided. Rhodesian tempers were the shorter as these columns were being welcomed by the villagers. Another dangerous situation was developing over the refusal of a large ZANLA group to move towards an assembly point north of Salisbury.

By the end of the third day, 1800 armed men had reported to the rendezvous points. Relations with the monitoring force were tense, the guerrillas remaining to be convinced that they were not hand-in-glove with the Rhodesians. At this stage the monitoring teams changed their *modus operandi*. At still greater risk, they began to go into the bush with the Patriotic Front liaison officers to identify groups and bring them in. The difficulties were compounded by land-mines around many of the rendezvous points. A bus carrying guerrillas to an assembly place struck one of their own land-mines, killing some and wounding many more.

The numbers reporting crept up to 4280 at the end of the fifth and to 5640 by the end of the sixth day. There was some ZIPRA movement across the Zambesi east of Lake Kariba and through Botswana but, relatively, this was on a small scale. Fernando Honwana arrived as the representative of President Machel. Astonished at the orderliness and prosperity of Salisbury, he began forthwith to talk about the need for ZANU, whom he was convinced would win the elections, not to replicate the mistakes the FRELIMO government had made in Mozambique.

There was a lot of pressure to extend the assembly process. ZANU were pressing hard for this. We were not prepared to put the monitoring teams at further risk by extending the period in which they were exposed in 39 different locations. The period in which large armed bands were moving freely though the countryside could not last much longer without risk of serious incident. ZANLA clearly were using the period of disengagement to move their forces across the Mozambique border. Large groups showed no intention of moving to the assembly places until the last possible moment. A white farmer was murdered by a ZANLA group in the Penhalonga area. Battles had to be fought every day with the Rhodesian commanders to ensure that their forces did not reach to these large guerrilla movements. They had always seen great dangers in this period, when they were obliged to relinquish control. They would not have accepted a change in the terms of the cease-fire agreement. Above all, it was necessary to maintain the deadline if effective pressure was to be exerted on many of the armed groups now in the countryside to report to the assembly areas.

Soames, therefore, rejected calls for any formal extension of the assembly period. At the same time, we worked out with General Walls an understanding that movement from the rendezvous points to the assembly area would take place in secure conditions over the next 48 hours. These arrangements were not announced, as this would have reduced the pressures on the Patriotic Front forces to assemble on time.

These tactics worked. The Patriotic Front commanders broadcast last-minute appeals to their forces to assemble. On the last day 5700 guerrillas reported to the rendezvous points – as many as had appeared in the whole of the previous six days – and several thousand more guerrillas assembled or began to do so over the next 48 hours. At one rendezvous point the Coldstream Guards found themselves with 1000 ZANLA to move to an assembly point in the Sabi tribal trust land. The numbers in that assembly place swelled eventually to 6000. With the British monitoring team there never more than 50 strong, there was a good deal of movement in and out of this assembly place and disturbances in the area throughout the period up to the elections.

By the end of the assembly process, the situation looked a great deal more promising than had appeared likely three days before. The Front had assembled a very large proportion of their forces. The count by this stage was over 15 000 men. A number of armed bands remained at large and the process inevitably had been accompanied by a fair amount of lawlessness and intimidation. Under pressure from the Rhodesian commanders, Soames authorized the deployment of Rhodesian forces at points on the Mozambique border where there was incontrovertible evidence of large-scale cross-border movement. The Rhodesians never had been able to control such movement, however, and the main ZANLA effort had been made well before the assembly process ended.

Soames, with undisguised relief, congratulated the members of the monitoring force on a brilliant feat of courage and organization. He paid tribute to the efforts of the Patriotic Front commanders and liaison officers. The Rhodesian forces and police also had acted with discipline and restraint. But the next few days were no less charged with danger. A number of large armed bands which had been identified were still refusing to report. It had been made clear at Lancaster House that if guerrilla bands remained in the field with their weapons, the Rhodesian forces would have to be authorized to deal with them. The general ZIPRA record of compliance with the cease-fire remained good. Few incidents were being reported from Matabeleland. At an assembly point west of Bulawayo, what amounted to a fully formed ZIPRA battalion had appeared.

Dabengwa now reported to Soames' staff that several hundred more ZIPRA were trying to assemble. Walls agreed that they must be given time to do so. On the ZANLA side, thanks to heroic efforts by the liaison officers, a number of other outstanding bands were talked in. By these means a further 5000 men were brought in between 5 and 9 January 1980, bringing the total in the camps to over 20 000. Despite a good deal of movement in and out of the assembly places, the numbers thereafter remained fairly steady, rising slightly – to 22 000 – by the time of the elections.

Great difficulty had been experienced in bringing in one ZANLA group, led by a particularly aggressive individual who would not respond to the orders of his own commanders, in the Belingwe area. The Rhodesians who, so far, had acted with restraint – thanks largely to the efforts of the monitoring force – gave repeated warnings that they would take military action if this group did not comply. After four days of fruitless negotiation, the Rhodesian commanders ordered an air-strike. The Rhodesian planes were unable to respond because of bad weather. By the time it cleared the ZANLA leader had at last been prevailed upon to move his men to an assembly point.

The groups now outstanding were extremely aggressive and showed no intention of joining the assembly process. On 10 January, with no monitoring force personnel present, the inevitable happened as an incident at Lupane got out of control. Twenty-eight dissident ZIPRA guerrillas made an armed incursion into the town and refused to hand over their weapons or be taken to the nearest assembly place. In an exchange of fire with the police, seven were killed. The ZIPRA commanders reacted calmly to this incident. Dissident groups in the area had been disobeying their orders for some time. Dabengwa suggested that ZIPRA units from the assembly places should be sent to deal with them. This was the only incident involving serious loss of life since the cease-fire, a period in which over 20 000 armed men in varying states of discipline and organization had moved across the country to the assembly places. To most of those in Rhodesia at the time the wonder was that no other and more serious incidents had occurred.

By this time ZIPRA had brought about 6500 men into the assembly areas. There appeared to have been a near-complete assembly of their forces, leaving no more than a few hundred men inside the country unaccounted for. The Zambesi, once again, had made cross-border movement difficult for them, as did the fact that the battalions left behind in Zambia with heavy equipment were organized on conventional lines. The cease-fire was proving generally effective in most areas of Matabeleland.

In the eastern provinces the situation was different. This was attributable in part to the differences in character between the two guerrilla armies. ZIPRA were well armed and had received conventional training, much of it provided, so far as the senior ranks were concerned, by East German and other East European instructors. ZANLA were relatively ill-armed and ill-equipped. They had received virtually no conventional training. They had far less of a hierarchal structure. All those willing to fight were given a weapon; and weapons training in many cases was primitive. In the camps accidental discharges were common, resulting in some deaths and more casualties. Yet it was ZANLA who had done the bulk of the fighting. Although some fringe groups were engaged mainly in banditry and were outside any effective control, the bulk of the ZANLA forces had been effectively politicized and, as the assembly process had shown, their command structure was far more effective than the Rhodesians had appreciated.

Towards the end of the assembly process, on 5 January an appalling incident occurred. A Rhodesian District Commissioner and his assistant, after a two-day drinking bout, opened fire from their car on any Africans they encountered, killing two people and injuring several more. They were arrested and charged with murder.

The situation in and around the assembly places remained tense throughout the transition. On several occasions members of the monitoring force had weapons pointed at them. In the worst case ZANLA surrounded the entire Australian contingent in one assembly point with machine-guns, rocket-launchers and mortars trained on them. Their fears of attack could be kept under control – provided the Rhodesian police and other forces could be dissuaded from patrolling in close proximity to the camps. In mid-January the Rhodesians conducted an operation against an 'outstanding' ZANLA group dangerously close to one assembly place and positioned mortars on a hill overlooking another. Following remonstrances by the monitoring force, these were removed. Later in the cease-fire, a Rhodesian detachment which got too close to another assembly place was overrun by ZANLA. It was fortunate for both sides that there were no casualties in an incident which, like many others, could rapidly have turned into a dangerous confrontation. In the only mixed assembly point, in south Matabeleland, the ZIPRA and ZANLA contingents exchanged mortar fire one night. The Patriotic Front commanders flew down from Salisbury and an uneasy peace was restored.

10 Tension

Soames and his staff now faced two related problems. The first was the continuing high level of incidents attributable to outstanding ZANLA groups. The second was the attitude of the Rhodesian commanders. They had scarcely anticipated ending the assembly process with the Front still in the settlement – expecting ZANLA in particular either to make no effort to assemble the majority of their forces, or undisciplined units to start fighting the monitoring force. They protested that ZANLA had used the period of disengagement to move large numbers of men across the Mozambique border, in violation of the cease-fire agreement. Soames had already authorized a Rhodesian deployment along the eastern border. Appeals were also made to the government of Mozambique. But they were no more able than the Rhodesians to control much of the border; and they wanted as many ZANLA as possible inside Rhodesia.

But ZANLA had delivered no fewer than 14 000 men to the assembly places, thereby countering effectively any criticism of a failure to assemble their forces and, furthermore, demonstrating their numerical superiority to ZIPRA. The Rhodesians contended that a high proportion of the ZANLA forces who had assembled were women or teenage guerrilla scouts – *mujibas* – armed only with ancient weapons or stick grenades. 'Any self-respecting terrorist', claimed Peter Walls, 'has an AK 47!' On the ZANLA side, this was not strictly true. They did not have ZIPRA's access to Soviet and East German supplies. But the Rhodesian police were producing evidence that a considerable number of ZANLA sections had been instructed to remain in the field and to ensure that the villagers voted for ZANU. This evidence was based on interrogation by the Rhodesian police of captured ZANLA personnel and was corroborated when they were seen by British police advisers. It was greeted at first with suspicion at Government House as fitting far too neatly into the Rhodesian campaign to get Mugabe excluded from the elections. Mugabe, meanwhile, had compiled a list of his own complaints. From Maputo he sent an open letter to Mrs Thatcher pointing out that South African forces had not yet withdrawn from Rhodesia. ZANU would not allow their forces to be encircled. The auxiliaries had not been confined to their bases.

Soames made clear that he had no intention of excommunicating ZANU. They had assembled a very substantial proportion of their forces. But he was concerned at the evidence that other ZANLA sections had been instructed to remain in the field. At the same time he was receiving a stream of complaints about the auxiliaries. The monitoring force were instructed to pay particular attention to their activities.

Despite continuing incidents in the eastern tribal trust lands the level of violence had fallen significantly in most parts of the country. The RAF reported that white farmers were beginning to drive throughout the day in areas where, two weeks before, movement was well-nigh impossible. Rhodesia gradually was returning to normal. The Rhodesian Combined Operations Headquarters, however, were determined to try to give the contrary impression. They continued to pour out communiqués which, far from reflecting the fact that, over most of the country, the cease-fire was holding, inflated such incidents as were still continuing. Great prominence was given to reports of cattle-theft, there being fewer more serious incidents to report. These absurd communications were products of the 'psychological operations' branch of the Rhodesian forces which continued to pour out inept propaganda right up to the elections.

The Zimbabwe-Rhodesia Broadcasting Service, having been in the habit of taking its instructions from the Rhodesian Front, had since got used to doing so from the Rhodesian military. The local 6 p.m. news was replaced by that of the BBC World Service. The radio and television were required to give equal broadcasting time to all the parties participating in the elections. A BBC team were brought out to offer their advice. The election coverage was strictly controlled by the Election Commission. More could not be done about the treatment of other subjects without Soames and his staff in turn transforming themselves into censors, which we were not prepared to do.

The next task was to bring back the Patriotic Front political leaders and enable them to conduct their campaigns. There were serious worries about their security. The white community had not forgotten the shooting down by Nkomo's forces of two civil aircraft and the massacre of most of the survivors in one of those incidents. There had been explicit threats to kill Nkomo on his return. The whites had also been presented by the regime with a caricature of Mugabe as a kind of Marxist ogre. At his request, Nkomo was provided with British police protection. Since the Lancaster House agreement, he had made a series of statements about national reconciliation. Gradually these did change the attitude of the whites towards him. Muzorewa held a major rally in the Zimbabwe Grounds stadium in Salisbury on 6 January. It was now Nkomo's turn. He returned on the following Sunday and was taken by police helicopter to address a rally attended by over 100 000 people – a good many of them brought by bus from Bulawayo.

The ZANU leaders except Mugabe by this stage had arrived from Maputo. The original intention had been that Mugabe should address his rally on Sunday 20 January. Sithole had proceeded to book the stadium on that day, though something a good deal more modest would have sufficed to accommodate his few thousand supporters. He also attempted, through the courts, to obtain an injunction debarring Mugabe's party from using the name ZANU. Soames intervened to stay this procedure, enabling Mugabe's party to register itself as ZANU (PF) for the elections.

Another problem remained to be resolved. While Soames had ordered the release of all political prisoners within Rhodesia, ZANU had not yet fulfilled their undertaking to release their own detainees – 60 or so 'dissenters' who, having fallen out with the ZANU leadership, were imprisoned in Mozambique. Although they were of no political significance, they too had the right to freedom and had succeeded in getting petitions to the British government demanding their release. In another exercise in brinkmanship, ZANU and the Mozambicans were told that these prisoners must be released by the time Mugabe returned to Salisbury.

The difficulties Soames was to experience with white opinion in Rhodesia were demonstrated from the outset, when his decision to commute to life-imprisonment the death-sentences imposed on 11 common-law criminals convicted of murder provoked an outcry in the local press and on the part of Rhodesian Front politicians. The great majority of the white population feared that if the elections bought ZANU to power, they would not abide by the constitution. There would be trials and purges and no future for them. Nor were these anxieties confined to the whites. Village headmen and other 'collaborators' had been killed throughout the war. A year before, ZANU in Maputo had broadcast a 'death list' of politicians involved in the internal settlement. A good many of them felt that they would be lucky to keep their heads on their shoulders if ZANU won.

The argument about an additional assembly place for the Patriotic Front forces had resulted in a virtual rupture of Soames' relations with General Walls: they barely spoke again until the eve of independence. Duff and I had regular meetings with the Rhodesian commanders. By the third week of January, relations with them were moving towards a crisis. They were not persuaded of the value of a peaceful settlement if it included ZANU. There was talk of returning to the war and appealing for South African assistance. Some of the senior Rhodesian civilians were very worried by their attitude. The danger of this situation was that the Rhodesian military did not need to organize a coup. It would have sufficed for them to have organized a breakdown of the ceasefire. The danger of ZANLA conduct was that it was offering them pretexts to do so. In response to movement by the guerrillas in and out of the assembly places, the Rhodesians had ordered their forces to patrol within the buffer zone around the assembly areas.

Soames had no intention of giving in to Rhodesian demands to ban ZANU. Apart from destroying all possibility of international acceptance of the elections, such action would have placed in the greatest possible danger the British and Commonwealth teams in the assembly areas, as well as bringing an immediate resumption of the war. Our strategy had to be not to drive ZANU out of the settlement, but to apply enough pressure on them and others to enable the country to get through to the elections with all parties still present in them. The Rhodesians were told again that ZANU would not be banned, but that Soames intended to increase the pressure on all the parties to comply with the Lancaster House agreement. That included disciplining the auxiliaries. If the country was to have any prospect of a peaceful future, planning must begin for the integration of the forces after the elections.

On 21 January the Rhodesian commanders held a meeting to decide whether to proceed with the settlement. The Treasury Secretary, David Young, who had consulted his civilian colleagues, told the military commanders that a failure to do so would have disastrous consequences for Rhodesia. He was supported by Ken Flower. By this time Walls also had come round to the side of the moderates. He assured me that he had no intention of letting Rhodesian forces get so close to the assembly points as to cause a breakdown of the cease-fire.

After these successes, first in consolidating the cease-fire and then in overcoming this crisis with the Rhodesian military, our next priority was to deal with the question of the South African forces on Rhodesian territory. During the Lancaster House Conference it was common knowledge that several hundred South African military personnel were in Rhodesia. The Rhodesian forces depended on the equipment they received from South Africa. The Rhodesian delegation at Lancaster House had made clear that they would not enter into any agreement which did not permit these supplies to continue. They were reassured on that score. But they also were told that it would not be possible for formed units of the South African forces to remain in Rhodesia under a British Governor. The same message was given to the South African government. In the Conference, the Patriotic Front sought assurances about the South African forces. They were told that there would be no external intervention in Rhodesia under a British Governor. At the same time Carrington made clear that, pending the elections, there would be no attempt at a purge of individual military personnel on either side. The Rhodesians were not the only ones to be receiving help of this kind. During the assembly process 500 FRELIMO soldiers appeared with ZANLA and in due course were repatriated to Mozambique.

On arriving in Salisbury, we discovered, not entirely to our surprise, that the picture was not as the Rhodesians had painted it. The Rhodesians revealed that there was in fact a South African company on Rhodesian territory on the north side of the bridge across the Limpopo at Beit Bridge. They refused to accept the withdrawal of this company, at any rate in the period in which it was far from clear whether there would be an effective cease-fire at all. If the South African presence could not be removed at once, Soames was determined that it should be declared. On 6 January his spokesman announced that the South African company would remain for the time being on Rhodesian territory for the sole purpose of protecting the bridge, which was the essential communications link between South Africa, Rhodesia and Zambia.

This produced an international outcry. The Patriotic Front also criticized this state of affairs, though their criticism was more muted. This was because their main interest was in seeing whether we would prove able to secure the withdrawal of the South African contingents and they had little faith in the ability of external critics to do so. The outcry was something Soames was prepared to face because he regarded it as preferable to an attempt to disguise the truth; and because he had other priorities at this stage. However offensive the South African presence appeared at the United Nations, it seemed less important at the time within Rhodesia than whether the cease-fire could be made to take effect at all. Public demands by Soames for a South African withdrawal would have been followed by a South African refusal to continue providing the supplies on which the Rhodesian forces depended; and that in turn would have resulted in the withdrawal of their support for a settlement. With relations with the Rhodesian commanders already under the most serious strain, any peremptory action would have led to a breakdown. While South African *approval* was never sought for anything the British government did – and indeed they very clearly disapproved of most of it – South African *acquiescence* had to be secured if their influence was not to be exerted against proceeding with the elections.

The time to deal with the South African troop presence had now come, the more so as it appeared that a unit on the south-east border also was composed of South African personnel. The Rhodesians were reminded of the requirement that there must be no South African units on Rhodesian territory under a British administration. They argued that the South African presence was essential to secure their supply routes. In reality Walls regarded the presence of these forces as a guarantee of South African support. His concern was to keep South Africa tied into the defence of Rhodesia. Once withdrawn, he reasoned, it was unlikely that they would return. This, of course, was true, and rendered it necessary to deal direct with the South Africans.

Sir Antony Duff was despatched to Cape Town to see President Botha, who agreed to announce that the South African contingent would hand over responsibility for the protection of Beit Bridge to the Rhodesians. But this did not put an end to the South African military presence in Rhodesia. Five or six hundred South African military personnel remained, some of them more or less integrated in the Rhodesian forces. Immediately the election results were known, there was an exodus of the remaining South African personnel and much South African supplied equipment. But this problem too had been reduced in scope sufficiently for it no longer to impede progress towards the elections.

By this time, ZANU had agreed to release the detainees in Mozambique. Sithole's rally had been a fiasco. On the following Sunday, 27 January, Mugabe returned to Salisbury and addressed a meeting of 150 000 people – easily the largest of the rallies addressed by the three major political leaders. As I drove through the city that morning, virtually the entire African youth of Salisbury seemed to be heading for the Zimbabwe Grounds. The rally demonstrated conclusively the hold that ZANU had established in and around the capital, as well as in the rural areas.

No one was more conscious of the imperfections of his administration than Soames. He was not in a position simply to impose his views. Military power remained in the hands of the Rhodesian commanders. It was necessary to proceed through a continual process of negotiation with them. This imposed a considerable strain on all concerned. It also meant that results took time to achieve; but in the end they were achieved. The police, who had long resented their increasing subordination to the Rhodesian army under the martial law regime, in general were co-operating well. So were the heads of the civil service. What amounted to a continuous parallel negotiation was conducted at the same time with the Patriotic Front. In personal terms Soames found it easy to get on with Nkomo. Relations with Muzorewa were at a low ebb. Despite plenty of money, much of it from South Africa, he was running a singularly inept campaign. The response he got was poor and his reaction was to blame most of his difficulties on Soames and his administration. Meetings with Mugabe were dominated at the time by the need to get outstanding ZANLA elements to report to the assembly places and cease intimidation in the rural areas. These exchanges, although more highly publicized, were no more tense than some of those taking place with the Rhodesian military.

Despite these and other difficulties, in seven weeks much had been accomplished. Throughout most of the country the cease-fire was holding. The situation of the 22 000 Patriotic Front guerrillas in the assembly places had been stabilized and relations with the monitoring force were improving. All the border crossing points with Zambia and Mozambique, closed for years during the war, had been re-opened. Two hundred thousand tons of maize were on their way to Zambia. A good start had been made with the repatriation of the quarter of a million Zimbabwean refugees in Zambia, Botswana and Mozambique. Mugabe and Nkomo had returned and were campaigning actively. Our preoccupations at this stage were with reducing ZANLA activity to levels at which it would no longer threaten a Rhodesian military reaction; getting through to the elections with all parties present in them; dealing with the situation which would arise in the assembly areas immediately the election results were known; and trying to pave the way for the merger of the forces which must then be accomplished if future stability was to be assured.

On 2 February the UN Security Council turned its attention to Rhodesia, passing a resolution which called for the withdrawal of South African forces and the confinement of the Rhodesian forces to their bases, failing which, it was suggested, the Lancaster House agreement would be in danger of collapse. The resolution took little account of the terms of the cease-fire agreement, the fact that the British administration had been successful in stopping the war or of the difficulties which had to be overcome in implementing the settlement. The British representative, Sir Anthony Parsons, pointed out that for years the international community had been urging Britain to assume direct responsibility for Rhodesia. It had now done so, and in exercising that responsibility we would be guided by the terms of the agreement we had negotiated. It was not open to either side to select only those elements it found to its taste. Success or failure would be decided in Rhodesia. The British delegation declined to participate in the vote.

In Salisbury, this seemed the least of Soames' problems. Nkomo had been prevented by ZANU from holding a meeting in Umtali. Muzorewa by now was threatening to withdraw from the Lancaster House agreement. The threat did not carry much conviction. But Muzorewa also had been prevented from holding a meeting in his home area of Manicaland. Intimidation was not a practice confined to one party. In Sithole's case, it was the support rather than the desire that was lacking. Muzorewa's youth wing had organized attacks on ZANU candidates in Salisbury. It had long since ceased to be paying to support anyone other than ZAPU in Matabeleland. ZANU, however, were rendering it hard for any other party to campaign in the eastern provinces. In most of the rural areas, they had established their dominance.

The British at the time estimated that in addition to fringe elements outside any effective control, about 2000 to 3000 ZANLA remained in the field. This was an underestimate. ZANLA proved subsequently to have kept 7000 men outside the assembly places. Intimidation was not an abstract concept. It book the form mostly of threats, but also of the murder, mutilation or abduction of those campaigning for or suspected of sympathizing with other parties. A few exemplary punishments of this kind were sufficient to discourage others. This violence did not spread to the townships. Nkomo joined Muzorewa in protesting that he was unable to campaign anywhere in rural Mashonaland. He held a press conference to complain at the abduction of several of his party workers and the murder of one of his parliamentary candidates by ZANLA. He was last seen having red-hot coals forced down his throat.

11 Transition

Soames consulted the British officials in all regions of Rhodesia. They reported that in the eastern tribal trust lands there had been intimidation over a long period. All the parties were able to campaign freely in the towns. All of Matabeleland was Nkomo territory, but other parties were able to operate. There were continuing complaints about the behaviour of the auxiliaries. But it could hardly be argued that free and fair elections could be held in areas where only one party was able to campaign.

As well as Nkomo and Muzorewa, Ian Smith now wanted to know what Soames proposed to do. In his *démarche*, Soames detected undertones of a white coup. The danger of others seeking to take some action of their own was increasing. At Lancaster House all the delegations had been told that if any party practised widespread intimidation, Soames would take action. The only existing powers enabled him to ban a party as a whole from participating in the elections. This Soames had no intention of doing, but he did need to increase his leverage on ZANU and others to comply. Soames therefore now promulgated two ordinances enabling him to take selective action. On 9 February the ZANLA commander, Rex Nhongo, was persuaded to make a broadcast calling on outstanding ZANLA forces to report to the assembly areas. This produced no response. On the same day Soames took action to prevent a ZANU candidate, Enos Nkala, from campaigning, though not from standing, in the elections. Nkala had been saying, even more clearly than other ZANU candidates, that if ZANU did not win, the war would continue. This action was taken *pour encourager les autres*.

Based on reports from the British officials in the regions, maps were published indicating those areas in which acts of political violence and threats against voters had been such that, so far, campaigning could not be freely undertaken. We made clear that a marked improvement was looked for to enable fair elections to be held in these areas.

Acts of violence and intimidation were by no means con-

fined to ZANU. Following the attack on 22 December on
the house of Mugabe's sister, on 5 February a ZANU candidate, Kangai, was wounded in a rocket attack on his home
by members of Muzorewa's youth wing. The same group
threw a grenade at Mugabe's house in Salisbury. On 9 February the former Prime Minister and leading opponent of
Ian Smith, Garfield Todd, was arrested by the police in
Shabani because a schoolmaster on his farm had helped a
member of ZANLA. We secured his immediate release and
the dropping of the charges against him. But this was not
the last exploit of the Shabani police. On 13 February Richard
Hove, Julia Zvobgo and another ZANU candidate were arrested and charged with contacts with ZANLA personnel
outside the assembly places. These incidents were unchar-
acteristic of the general attitude of the police. Although they
did not much like what was happening, in general they co-
operated with Soames and his administration, applying the
new laws as they had the old. Many of them were delighted
no longer to have to take orders from the army. The Police
Commissioner, Peter Allum, served on for a year under
Mugabe; and Richard Hove became Minister for the Public
Service in Mugabe's first government.   ·

On 10 February there occurred an incident of an entirely
different order, and by far the most serious of the transition. As Mugabe was leaving an election meeting in Fort
Victoria, a mine was exploded by remote control in an attack on his car. Mugabe came within a hair's breadth of
being killed. The Police Commissioner was infuriated – the
more so as Mugabe had been provided with a police escort
who certainly would also have been killed. Unlike the others,
this attempt almost certainly had been organized by elements
of the Rhodesian special forces and their South African
counterparts. At what level it had been ordered, it was impossible at the time to determine. Walls denied all knowledge. If the Rhodesian army had been determined to kill
Mugabe, they would have succeeded, he told Duff and me
and, for that matter, Mugabe himself.

On the following evening explosions took place outside
three churches in Salisbury. A fourth bomb failed to go off,
while 'evidence' nearby was intended to implicate ZANU.
Lieutenant Edwin Piringondo and another member of the

Selous Scouts blew themselves up in a car on the same evening. The police had no doubt that they were responsible for the bombings. On the eve of the elections a bomb attack was made on the pro-Patriotic Front journal *Moto*. Combined Operations Headquarters, meanwhile, persisted in issuing communiqués as if the war was continuing. At the level of comedy the 'psychological operations' branch of the Rhodesian forces continued to produce and distribute pamphlets proclaiming the virtues of 'true democracy', with propaganda hostile to the Patriotic Front. With characteristic incompetence, bundles of these pamphlets were dropped by air on members of the Commonwealth observer team sent to Rhodesia to witness the elections!

On 17 February at the last minute Mugabe cancelled plans to address a rally in Bulawayo because of suspicions, which may have been well-founded, that a further attempt might be made to assassinate him there.

The other main theme of this period was the attempt to persuade the Rhodesian commanders to plan for the integration of their forces and those of the Front, failing which the outcome of the elections would quickly have been overtaken by a resumption of the war. This was a problem which, Walls apart, the Rhodesian commanders in Salisbury seemed determined to try to disregard – other than advancing various impracticable schemes for the demobilization of the Patriotic Front forces.

Our minds were concentrated by the fact that the moment of maximum danger for the monitoring force was liable to come as soon as the result of the elections was known. Whatever the result, it was certain to cause problems in some at least of the assembly places. General Acland declared his intention of withdrawing the monitoring teams from the assembly places immediately the elections were completed – and before the results were declared. This would have led to the immediate dispersal of the guerrilla forces back into the bush. General Acland had come to this view largely in frustration at the refusal of the Rhodesian commanders to think or plan ahead and in an attempt to force them to do so. Indeed, he believed at this stage that some of the monitoring teams might have to fight their way out while the guerrillas dispersed.

Walls at least could see the need to avoid a dénouement of this kind. By the end of January, joint police and Patriotic Front patrols were operating around some of the assembly places. After several meetings with him, in mid-February Nkomo told me that he agreed that a ZIPRA battalion should move to the Essexvale Barracks outside Bulawayo to receive training from the Rhodesian army, under the auspices of the monitoring force. With great difficulty, Walls was persuaded that a similar offer must be made to ZANLA. Mugabe accepted this at once. A ZANLA battalion also was designated to receive training. Mugabe added that he considered it essential that the monitoring force should remain in the country after the election to provide stability, preside over the integration of the forces and train the new Zimbabwe army. After a series of difficult meetings, this was the moment at which a strong personal relationship began to be established between Soames and Mugabe.

On 19 February, with the elections just eight days away, General Acland proposed that the cease-fire commission, with representatives of the commanders on both sides, should visit the assembly places to instruct the guerrilla forces to remain in them after the elections and assure them that they would be incorporated in the future Zimbabwe army. Walls responded by offering to tour the assembly areas with Nkomo and Mugabe. A small permanent Rhodesian police presence by this stage had been established, with the help of the monitoring teams, in each of the assembly areas; and the Rhodesians began to take over the task of supplying them. Nkomo agreed to visit the ZIPRA assembly places to instruct his men to remain in them and accept the Rhodesian presence. Mugabe's deputy, Muzenda, gave similar instructions to ZANLA. General Acland agreed with the other Commonwealth contingents that they would withdraw from the assembly places on 3 March – the day before the election results would be known. But small British monitoring teams would remain in all the assembly places during the crucial week following the elections.

The Rhodesian Front, meanwhile, had won all 20 seats in the elections on 14 February for the white members of Parliament. In most cases their candidates were returned unopposed. The white electorate, it appeared, had learned nothing and forgotten nothing. They seemed not to attribute to Ian Smith and his party any of the problems which beset the country.

The various limited actions taken *vis-à-vis* ZANU appeared to be having some effect. The areas still seriously affected by violence had been reduced to sectors on the north-east border, part of Manicaland and much of Victoria province. In these areas violence was continuing at much the same level as before the cease-fire. About 10 per cent of the voting population was affected.

On 22 February, five days before the elections, Soames held a further meeting with the British officials in the provinces. They reported that the spreading out into the countryside of the security forces, reinforced by the call-up for the election period of the reservists, was helping to reduce intimidation. In some of the areas in which this had been impossible before, all parties had been able to hold meetings. Intimidation had had its effect in many areas, but the virtually unanimous view was that this would not justify the abrogation or deferment of polling.

On the basis of their report, Soames concluded that it made no sense to suspend or defer polling in any part of the country. Following the attack on him at Fort Victoria, Mugabe had cancelled all further public meetings. Having been nearly blown up himself, with one of his candidates wounded, three others detained and the Selous Scouts trying to attribute to ZANU crimes for which elements of the Rhodesian forces were in fact responsible, it was now Mugabe who had grounds to complain. Muzorewa, however, was reported to be summoning a meeting of his delegation at Lancaster House; and question-marks remained about the attitude of the Rhodesian military.

Fernando Honwana had arranged for Walls and Flower to be invited to visit Mozambique. The Mozambican Chief of Defence Staff welcomed Walls on what he described as his first legal visit to his country: Walls, as Army Commander, had been in the habit of participating in the cross-border operations of his forces. The Mozambicans argued that Mugabe was not a Marxist. Why did the Rhodesians never talk to him? Walls said that he was ready to talk to Mugabe, as he was to Nkomo, if Mugabe wanted this. The Mozambicans offered to help arrange such a meeting.

The British team, over the weekend, told the Rhodesians that Soames had no intention of taking action of a kind which would affect international acceptance of the election result or drive ZANU back to the war. Nor did he see any sense in taking action on a limited scale to suspend or postpone polling in some areas, which inevitably would be seen as arbitrary, while making little difference to the result. This message was more readily received by some than others. The Rhodesian attitude at this stage was influenced by their own assessment of the likely outcome of the elections. This seemed to be based mainly on reports from the special branch of the police. They had no doubt that a high proportion of the population in the Shona tribal trust lands would vote for ZANU. But they believed that a majority of people in the towns and African labour on the European farms would support Muzorewa. While forecasting accurately the extent of Nkomo's support, they believed that ZANU and Muzorewa would divide the Shona votes about equally between them.

We were sceptical of the Rhodesian assessment – to the extent that we shared the view of virtually all other observers that ZANU would win the largest number of seats. It did not, however, seem probable to anyone except Fernando Honwana, who gave me an exact prediction of the result, that ZANU by themselves would be able to win over 50 seats. There were no opinion polls; and if any had been organized, they would have been of no value. The African population had long since learned to disguise their opinions – above all from the authorities and from their employers. It had been possible to get to this point in large part because all three major parties believed that they still had a chance of winning. As we pointed out on the eve of the elections, none of those who had accused the British administration of bias in one direction or another were able with any confidence to predict the result. Julius Nyerere seemed to find this uncertainty unsettling. He announced that he would only recognize the result if the Patriotic Front won!

On 25 February Muzorewa organized a meeting of his former government in the house of Ian Smith. The purpose was to consider whether they should declare the agreement they had entered into in London null and void; demand that the elections be postponed; or seek in some way to re-establish the former government, perhaps with some offer to Nkomo. Ian Smith argued that the elections should be postponed. Walls and Flower were summoned to this meeting. Walls declared himself in favour of proceeding with the elections. Since this group could do nothing without the army, his influence was decisive in checking any move to denounce the Lancaster House agreement. The other factor appears to have been an optimistic assessment from Rhodesian intelligence sources of Muzorewa's chances in the townships and among the large African labour force in the European farming areas. We had managed to get around this corner, albeit with screaming tyres.

On the same day we announced the transfer of the ZIPRA battalion to the Essexvale training camp near Bulawayo and that a similar offer had been made to ZANLA. The *New York Times* reported Soames as having taken Rhodesia to the 'brink of the improbable'. The accusations of bias had proved self-cancelling. By an exercise in brinkmanship and against most expectations, Soames had managed to get through to the elections with all parties present in them. Other commentators agreed, but pointed to the dangers of a military coup if ZANU won, and of a return to the war by ZANLA if they did not.

On the eve of the elections Soames asked Mugabe to call in an attempt to consolidate relations of greater confidence with him. Mugabe had agreed that the first ZANLA troops should move into training. Mugabe and Nkomo, overruling their respective military commanders, also agreed that the training should take place with Rhodesian weapons and equipment: as the guerrillas moved into the training camps, Kalashnikovs were handed over in return for Rhodesian-issue rifles. Soames told Mugabe that he was concerned about intimidation, but had no intention of disqualifying ZANU or postponing the elections in any part of the country. Mugabe said that he expected to win the elections. But there would need to be a coalition government. There must be Africanization, particularly of the civil service. But he would need time to take over the government of the country. He wanted Soames and the rest of us to stay for some months after the elections to help in this process and to maintain confidence.

On the same day, Walls also met Mugabe. The latter referred to the bomb explosions in Salisbury and the attempts to assassinate him. Walls said that he was not responsible for these incidents. He assured Mugabe that if ZANLA forces remained in the camps, the Rhodesians were not going to attack them. Mugabe said that some people thought that the Rhodesian forces might stage a coup. Walls said that they would not do so. Mugabe, not surprisingly, was unconvinced. On the next day he flew to Mozambique, returning to Salisbury at the weekend, after the polling had ended.

12 Independence

On 27 February, the first day of the elections, 1 375 000 people – nearly half the total electorate – voted. Soames and others who visited the polling stations detected the first signs of a ZANU landslide. ZANU supporters were active and vocal in the queues outside them. Polling continued at a rate far exceeding the high turnout in the Muzorewa elections a year before. The representative of the UN Secretary-General, later to become Secretary-General himself, Pérez de Cuéllar, told us that he had been extremely impressed by the conduct of the election. Like the world press, he seemed to find both picturesque and reassuring the presence in remote parts of the bush of British policemen, in helmets and shirt-sleeves, supervising the polling!

By the last day of polling there were many indications that the tide was running strongly in favour of Mugabe throughout Mashonaland. By the end of the three-day election, nearly 2.7 million had voted. From the regions there were reports of intimidation by ZANU in Victoria province; but over by far the greater part of the country voting had been taking place in normal conditions.

As the evidence accumulated of heavy voting for ZANU, attempts began to be made among the other parties to form some kind of anti-ZANU coalition. A government including Muzorewa, Nkomo and the whites was the Rhodesian objective. Our objective was the widest possible coalition: this was essential to the avoidance of an attempt by any party to return to the war.

There was much speculation as to whether Soames necessarily would call upon the leader of the largest party to form the new government. This was largely academic, a question of electoral arithmetic. The constitution stipulated that the Prime Minister designate should be the person who, in the opinion of the Governor, was best able to command the support of the majority of members of the House of Assembly. It had been agreed at Lancaster House that the votes of the 20 white MPs could not be used to form a government against the wishes of the African electorate. There could be no question of seeking to establish a government which depended for its majority on white support. If ZANU had fallen well short of winning an absolute majority of the 80 African seats, Nkomo would have had his chance of becoming Prime Minister, since both ZANU and Muzorewa might have agreed to co-operate with him, and certainly would not do so with each other. If ZANU won or got close to winning a majority of the African votes, then Mugabe certainly was going to be called upon to form a government.

The elections had been witnessed by a host of observers, including a British parliamentary delegation and teams appointed by almost all Western governments. Apart from that of Pérez de Cuéllar, who had formed a favourable opinion, the report of the Commonwealth observer group was likely to have the most impact on outside opinion. Soames called on all the observers present at the elections to make public their opinions before the results were known. Most of them did so. The conclusions of all the official groups were unanimously favourable, including that of the Commonwealth team.

Soames' main concern, however, was with the report of the British election supervisors, led by the Election Commissioner, Sir John Boynton. Their conclusion was that intimidation in some areas, particularly of Victoria province, had been such as to be likely to have distorted the pattern of voting. Overall, however, the elections in general were a fair reflection of the wishes of the people. Sir John Boynton's conclusion was that in the country as a whole the degree of intimidation and pressure was not so great as to invalidate the overall results of the poll.

This conclusion was not that of the Rhodesian military. On Saturday 1 March, the majority of the Rhodesian commanders in the Hurricane, Thrasher and Repulse operational areas, covering the north-east, east and south-east of the country, told Walls formally that in their opinion free and fair elections had not been held. The voters had been subjected to massive intimidation. The Governor should declare the elections null and void. He should continue to run the country with an all-party council.

That evening General Walls sent a message to Mrs Thatcher. Despite the assurances given at Lancaster House, he argued, action had not been taken to deal with intimidation. Walls asked the Prime Minister to declare the elections null and void.

On the morning of Sunday 2 March, Sir Antony Duff and I were asked to meet the Rhodesian commanders at Combined Operations Headquarters. They stated formally that they did not regard the election results as free and fair. Walls said that his attitude would depend on the response to his message to Mrs Thatcher. Duff and I said that the Election Commissioner's report would acknowledge that the results had been distorted by intimidation in some areas. But it concluded that the overall result broadly reflected the wishes of the people of Rhodesia. This was the Governor's view also. On the Rhodesian side there was concern that if Mugabe proved to have won an overall majority, there might be a period of chaos and a mass exodus of the whites.

Before a further meeting with the Rhodesian commanders that evening, Duff told Walls, on Mrs Thatcher's instructions, that there was no question of invalidating the results of the elections. The British election supervisors and other observers had reported that there had been intimidation in some areas. But their unanimous conclusion was that the elections were as free and fair as was possible in the circumstances and constituted a genuine expression of the will of the Zimbabwean people.

The Rhodesian military leaders continued to express regret that they had ever agreed to launch Rhodesia on such a course – though one or two had the grace to admit that they could not in any event have won the war. They argued strongly that the British could not simply walk away from the outcome. The British government must help to ease the transfer of power that was now about to take place. They were told that Soames would be working for the creation of as broadly based a coalition as possible.

Walls and the other commanders had behaved with dignity, despite their bitterness at the disaster that had hit them ('the enemy is about to become our government'). Despite some wild talk about military action among the regional commanders, that danger seemed to be receding, and Walls' own influence was exerted against it. As he said later, he had considered the possibility, only to reject it. 'It might have lasted forty-eight hours or more. Many people would have been killed. It would have been a chaotic state of affairs.' As we pointed out to Walls at the time, it would have brought disaster to the white community, as well as to the country as a whole, as such exploits had in Algeria and, more recently, in Mozambique. The transition we were attempting now to organize was intended, among other things, to give white Rhodesians time to choose whether they wanted to stay or to leave; to encourage many of them to stay; and to enable those who wished to do so to leave in good order, at a time of their own choosing.

On the following day, Walls took the other commanders to see Mugabe. That evening he made a statement on television urging people to accept the election results calmly.

There was no doubt, however, about the severity of the shock that would be felt by the white community, the security forces and Nkomo's supporters. Mugabe's landslide victory posed the problem that, although he had won the support virtually of the entire Shona-speaking population, he had no support in Matabeleland or with the whites. Nkomo had won the entire Ndebele vote. ZIPRA had 6000 armed men within the country and another 8000 in Zambia. The Rhodesian forces remained intact and were undefeated. Mugabe, conscious of these dangers, was conscious also that he was going to need British help to get his government established and its authority accepted.

On the morning of 4 March the election results were announced. Mugabe's party won 57 of the 80 African seats, giving it an absolute majority in the National Assembly. Support for Muzorewa had largely collapsed. He won half a million votes, but only three seats. Nkomo won all 20 seats in Matabeleland and none in the rest of the country.

Soames saw Mugabe immediately, congratulated him on his victory and asked him to form a government. Mugabe needed no convincing of the need to form a broadly based coalition and to do something to reassure the white community. Mugabe expressed appreciation of the role Soames had played. He noted that his party had no practical experience of government and pressed Soames again to stay for some months after the elections.

Soames saw Nkomo later in the morning and urged him

to take part in the new government. I told Honwana that Walls appeared willing to use his influence to help stabilize the situation. Machel was advising Mugabe strongly to take action to reassure the white population – to the extent, according to Mugabe, of suggesting that he should include Ian Smith in his government!

Walls had deployed troops at key points in Salisbury. This caused more alarm than reassurance. On the part of most of the white community the news was received in stunned silence.

Peter Walls wanted the British administration prolonged. We replied that we had a responsibility to ensure an orderly transition. The processes leading to independence would not be rushed. But the period of our responsibility could not be indefinitely prolonged. The Governor could not stay with no real authority. We would help, however, with military training after independence.

General Walls' personal distress was very great. Having been a hero to his forces and to the white community, he now found himself denounced by some of his own men, as well, of course, as by the Rhodesian Front. The reality, which he acknowledged, was that the war had long since ceased to be winnable from a Rhodesian point of view. If it had been, they never would have come to Lancaster House. Muzorewa's government never had been viable. There had been no real transfer of power, while the white community were unlikely to go on serving in the forces six months in every year on behalf of a 'black' government. Muzorewa's election had made no difference to the deterioration of the security situation. He had no influence on the 'boys' in the bush. Hence Ian Smith's repeated attempts to bring in Nkomo – but on Smith's terms. The Patriotic Front could not defeat the Rhodesian army and had suffered severely in almost every contact with them. But within a year or two they would have worn down the white community generally sufficiently to provoke some kind of collapse. Nor was it possible to explain the extent of Mugabe's election victory by intimidation. Virtually the entire Shona-speaking population had voted for him. Peter Walls acknowledged that many of his own forces must have done so.

In the evening, Mugabe made an eloquent broadcast.

'Greetings in the name of freedom', it began. His efforts, Mugabe said, would be directed towards the achievement of peace and stability. This was the time to beat swords into ploughshares. He would be inviting Nkomo to join his government, and also the representatives of other communities. His government would respect the constitution. It would not interfere with pensions, or individual property rights. General Walls would be authorized, working with the ZANLA and ZIPRA commanders, to preside over the integration of the forces. His government would bring change, but change could not occur overnight.

Mugabe told Soames again of his concern that independence should not be rushed. Soames explained that so long as he was Governor, he must remain exclusively responsible for the government. There could be no conflict of authority. Too long an interim would cause problems, as the new ministers naturally would wish to start exercising his authority. It was agreed that Soames would stay for six weeks, the date of independence being fixed for 18 April.

Mugabe discussed with Soames the formation of his government. To reassure the white community, he decided to appoint David Smith as Minister of Commerce and the President of the Rhodesian farmers' union, Denis Norman, as Minister of Agriculture. ZANU at first were disposed to offer Nkomo the presidency. He did not want this purely honorific post, and ZANU anyway had second thoughts. After difficult negotiations, Nkomo agreed to participate in the government as Minister for Home Affairs. Enos Nkala became Finance Minister. Bernard Chidzero was brought back from the United Nations to become Minister of Planning.

The Selous Scouts and some of the auxiliaries were melting away across the South African border. South African personnel and all loaned equipment had returned to South Africa. A substantial proportion of the whites in the police and army were making ready to leave. Most of those in the civil service realized that their posts were going to be Africanized. It was important that this inevitable run-down in the numbers of the white community – about 200 000 at the time of independence – should take place gradually if the handover was to be orderly and economic activity to be sustained. Public servants were able to take their pensions with them. Most of those engaged in business and commerce seemed disposed to stay. Reassured by the appointment of Denis Norman, so, for the time being, did most of the white farmers. This was crucial if Zimbabwe, hitherto a producer of surpluses, was not to become an importer of its own food. Mugabe wanted co-operatives to be established, but realized that it did not suffice to settle former guerrillas on a farm for any food to be produced. There were, at the time, more than enough vacant farms to be taken over. Samora Machel and Honwana counselled the new government not to emulate their experience in Mozambique, where an almost complete exodus of the white community brought a virtual breakdown of the economy.

The exodus of Rhodesian officers and NCOs was going to increase the need for military help from Britain. Soames was anxious also to prepare for an aid-donors' conference after independence. But no amount of aid would help if a British military training team were not established to help create a single army. Help was given with the reorganization of the civil service and the creation of a new Foreign Ministry. Soames was concerned that Britain should be prepared to do all this 'with some style, and ungrudgingly'. To that end, he visited London in mid-March. On his return, he was able to promise Mugabe substantial aid for reconstruction over the next three years.

But there were more immediate problems. Following the elections an additional 7000 ZANLA walked into the assembly places. These were the sections left in the countryside during the election campaign. The total in the assembly places was now 29 000. Walls was pressing ahead with demobilization of the auxiliaries and farm militias.

The Mozambican government had done much to help throughout the settlement. Honwana, in particular, had played a key role. On 24 March Soames visited Maputo as the guest of President Machel. Machel expressed his appreciation: the settlement would bring great benefits to his country. He hoped that Britain would be able to help with the rehabilitation of road and rail communications. The settlement, Soames concluded, had created the opportunity for Western governments to establish a better relationship with Mozambique.

Mugabe, meanwhile, was making clear that he had no

intention of becoming beholden to the Soviet Union. The Russians had never supplied him with arms. Mugabe considered that he owed them nothing. Relations were not improved by a suggestion, addressed to Nkomo, that a Soviet Deputy Foreign Minister should visit Zimbabwe before independence – an offer Mugabe turned down.

Relations with South Africa also required a lot of attention. Mugabe's victory had been greeted with dismay and there appeared to be two views on future policy towards Zimbabwe. The leaders of the security forces clearly thought it would serve South African interests to withdraw all cooperation, make life as difficult as possible for the new government and – given Zimbabwe's economic dependence on its links with South Africa – thereby demonstrate the supposed incapacity of an African government to run a country with any measure of success. The Foreign and Finance Ministries were prepared to take a more far-sighted view and to make some gestures intended to help establish a *modus vivendi* with the new regime.

This conflict of policy was never to be resolved until, years later, F.W. De Klerk took over as President of South Africa. But to help meet the short-term needs for foreign exchange, the South Africans agreed to make available soft loans which had been earmarked for the previous government. The South Africans' main concern was that Zimbabwe might become a base for attacks by members of the South African National Congress. Ninety members of the ANC had turned up in the ZIPRA assembly places. They were sent back to Zambia. Mugabe had attended Fort Hare University in the eastern Cape. The South African political system was a subject on which he had the strongest possible feelings. But he made clear that, while he would pursue the fight against apartheid by all political means, it was not possible for Zimbabwe, which had just emerged from seven years of war, to fight South Africa. He would invite no South African representatives to the independence ceremonies. Nor would he agree to diplomatic representation, though there could be a trade office. But the maintenance of economic links was essential. His government would support the liberation movements in all other ways, but could not afford to permit them to establish military bases in Zimbabwe.

With the Patriotic Front commanders, Walls by now had formed a joint military high command. The British team were determined to recover as many as possible of the ZIPRA forces in Zambia before independence. ZANU wanted them to return without their arms. Nkomo refused. It was agreed with Walls that the ZIPRA units should be allowed to retain their personal weapons; but their heavy equipment must be handed over to the government or the Zambians. It was thus possible to get most of the 8000 ZIPRA in Zambia back before independence, though the ZIPRA camp in Matabeleland near the Gwai river mine was to be the scene of trouble later. Mugabe had confirmed Walls' authority *vis-à-vis* the other commanders, though Walls made clear that he would not be prepared to undertake this task for long.

On 16 April the Prince of Wales arrived in Salisbury to represent the Queen at the independence celebrations. He was greeted by Soames, Walls and the ZANLA and ZIPRA commanders. On the following day he visited the Essexvale barracks where Patriotic Front forces were training with Rhodesian army personnel. Mrs Gandhi, President Kaunda, Malcolm Fraser and Dr Waldheim were among those who arrived to attend the independence celebrations. Peter Carrington represented the British Government.

There was one last alarm. As the heads of government gathered for a reception at Government House, Ken Flower reported to me the discovery of a cache of weapons in Salisbury, including rifles with telescopic sights. Mugabe's head of security, Emerson Munungagwa, was informed and security arrangements were tightened. But the plans for the ceremonies were not changed.

In his independence message to the people of Zimbabwe, Mugabe paid tribute to Soames for the role he had played in guiding the country to independence. 'His was from the outset a difficult and most unenviable task. . . . I am personally indebted to him for the advice he has given me on the art of managing the affairs of government.' Mugabe would, he said, be missing a good friend and counsellor, and so would the people of Zimbabwe.

At sunset on 17 April the Union Jack was hauled down in a simple ceremony in the grounds of Government House. The country was brought to independence at midnight in a ceremony attended by the Prince of Wales and delegations from over one hundred governments. Contingents from the three armies marched together in the parade. On the following day, Christopher Soames and his staff left Salisbury on the completion of his mission.

Part II
The End of Apartheid

13 The Afrikaners

Seven years later, when I arrived in Cape Town as the British Ambassador, the South African Foreign Minister, the indestructible Pik Botha, greeted me with the words: 'That was a terrible thing you did at Lancaster House!' When I enquired why, Pik Botha explained that, in his view, we had set the cause of reform in South Africa back by twenty years. If a 'moderate' black government had established itself in Zimbabwe, white South Africans would have been more open to political change. Half-expecting a greeting of this kind, I was able to reassure Pik Botha that wherever South Africa ended up, it was not going to be at Lancaster House.

I was despatched to South Africa by Margaret Thatcher because she felt that we needed to try to play a more active role. Britain, she was conscious, had more at stake there than any other country. We had by far the largest investments and, in that respect, the most to lose. Of the one-and-a-half million English-speaking white South Africans, we estimated that nearly a million either had or were entitled to British passports. The British government had begun to develop exaggerated worries as to what might happen if all or half of them decided to leave.

As in Rhodesia, the situation looked decidedly unpromising. In successive Commonwealth Conferences, the British government came under ever-increasing pressure to extend and intensify sanctions against South Africa. Margaret Thatcher held exactly the opposite view. 'I no more shared the established Foreign Office view of Africa than I did of the Middle East. . . . The basic, if usually unstated, assumption seemed to be that Britain's national interests required that we should ultimately be prepared to go along with the opinion of the radical black African states in the Commonwealth.'* She contended that the worst approach was to isolate South Africa further. This, in her view, contributed to an inflexible siege mentality on the part of the Afrikaners. Black South Africans had higher incomes than most blacks elsewhere in the

---

* Thatcher, op. cit., p. 512.

continent. Important British economic interests were at stake. She had no intention of throwing them away.

President P.W. Botha had introduced a number of reforms and there had been hopes that he might go further. When, in 1984, he visited Europe for the commemoration of the fortieth anniversary of the Normandy landings, Mrs Thatcher had invited him to Chequers. She 'did not particularly warm to' P.W. Botha, but she pressed him on independence for Namibia and the continued imprisonment of Nelson Mandela.

Botha's main 'reform' was the creation of a new Parliament in which the Indian and Coloured population were enabled to elect their own representatives in separate Houses. All real power remained with the white representatives. The white population voted strongly in favour of what they saw as incremental change. Yet, as Helen Suzman and others prophesied, the deliberate exclusion of the black population was bound to make matters worse. And so it proved, as resistance to the new Parliament exploded in the townships across the country.

In the summer of 1985, there came a real turning-point for South Africa. P.W. Botha was scheduled to make a speech which the more reformist members of his government characterized in advance as 'the crossing of the Rubicon'. When, on the advice of his security chiefs, he indicated instead an intention to maintain the *status quo*, accompanied by a crackdown on internal dissent, for the first time in its history really effective sanctions began to be applied to South Africa, not by any government, but by the financial markets. In its efforts to finance economic expansion, the South African government had accumulated large short-term foreign debts. When, in response to the 'Rubicon' speech, Chase Manhattan and the other US banks refused to roll over the short-term debts, they changed the course of South African history. The government was obliged to declare a moratorium before, eventually, being forced to agree to debt repayment terms which, combined with the reluctance of others to lend, forced South Africa into becoming a net *exporter* of capital.

At the Commonwealth summit in Nassau in October 1985, South Africa was the dominant issue. Mrs Thatcher opposed what she regarded as the Gadarene rush towards imposing further sanctions. Attacked for 'preferring British jobs to black lives', she countered that all the neighbouring African countries depended critically on the South African economy. She was prepared to agree no new sanctions except to ban the import of krugerrands and official trade promotion. 'As I entered the room, they all glared at me.'* In fact, from a domestic political point of view, Mrs Thatcher enjoyed these confrontations with the Commonwealth. For many of those criticizing the South African regime themselves were guilty of anti-democratic practices and the British public knew it.

Mrs Thatcher did agree at Nassau that the Commonwealth should send a group of 'eminent persons' to South Africa to report on the prospects for a conference. Geoffrey Howe declined to be drafted, correctly rating the chances of success as poor. When he protested that he was Foreign Secretary and could not do both jobs, Mrs Thatcher untactfully suggested that she could cope with his while he was away. Lord Barber instead was appointed to the group, led by Malcolm Fraser of Australia and General Obasanjo of Nigeria.

The group visited South Africa, meeting President Botha and his government and those black opposition figures still at large. They met the African National Congress in Lusaka and were permitted to visit Nelson Mandela in Pollsmoor prison near Cape Town. Having met representatives of most other shades of opinion, they put forward a 'possible negotiating concept' entailing the release of Mandela and all other political prisoners and the unbanning of the ANC and other parties. Pik Botha gave a conciliatory reply, but for P.W. Botha this was several bridges too far. On 19 May 1986, while the 'eminent persons' were still conducting their mission, the South Africans launched air-strikes against what they claimed to be ANC targets in Harare, Lusaka and Gaborone, effectively putting an end to the Commonwealth initiative.

It is a bitter irony and grim commentary on the respect for democratic rights elsewhere in Africa that today, while Nelson Mandela is President of South Africa, General Obasanjo – the outstanding member of the Commonwealth Eminent Persons group – languishes in jail as a political prisoner in Nigeria.

* Thatcher, op. cit., p. 518.

Following a European Community summit at The Hague in June 1986, Geoffrey Howe was despatched to South Africa to press for reform and the release of Mandela. He was extremely reluctant to go and, as Mrs Thatcher acknowledges, 'his reluctance proved justified since he was insulted by President Kaunda and brushed off by President Botha'.* The unfortunate Foreign Secretary was berated publicly on television by Kenneth Kaunda. Geoffrey Howe might have improved considerably his chances of becoming Prime Minister one day had he walked out. P.W. Botha received him in characteristically boorish fashion, only to reject his 'interference' as categorically as he had that of the Commonwealth group. The result was a special Commonwealth meeting in London at which Margaret Thatcher reluctantly agreed to some additional sanctions.

In sending me to South Africa, Mrs Thatcher knew that while I supported many of the sanctions which had been imposed, I did not support disinvestment. My experience of Africa was and is that it is easy to get foreign investors to leave, and far from easy to persuade them to return. I also felt that, through the presence of so many British citizens and as the largest foreign investor, we had a position of influence in South Africa and that we should try to use it more actively than, hitherto, we had seemed disposed to do. This was contrary to the received wisdom in the Foreign Office at the time where the sentiment was that we should keep our heads down and aim to engage in damage limitation. It was made clear to the South Africans that I was going there as the Prime Minister's appointment and that, I hoped, would give me some leverage with the regime: for they could hardly afford the complete withdrawal of her support, though they had been doing precious little to justify it.

For at the time, Mandela and most of his senior colleagues remained in prison with no prospect of release, the ANC and Pan African Congress (PAC) were banned, the press were heavily censored, a state of emergency was in force,

* Thatcher, op. cit., p. 520.

nearly all demonstrations of political dissent were suppressed and 2500 people were in detention without trial. It had to be said that these tactics were working in the sense that the crackdown was effective and 'order' had been restored. When I asked General Johann van der Merwe, head of the security police, why, on this occasion, the repression was proving successful, he replied cheerfully: 'This time we have arrested all the right people.'

The United Democratic Front (UDF) which, though it flatly denied it, represented the internal wing of the ANC, attempted to continue with demonstrations – quickly broken up by the police – and other forms of resistance. But its organization was weak, with all the real leaders in exile or in jail. Winnie Mandela and Allan Boesak continued to exercise an hypnotic influence on the Western press. Archbishop Tutu, with much greater moral authority, continued to campaign hard for the isolation of South Africa and general disinvestment.

Before arriving in South Africa, I had resolved to concentrate my efforts on the Afrikaners and the black leadership and to avoid falling into the easy trap of consorting mainly with the more liberal elements of the English-speaking community who, unfortunately and with one outstanding exception, were even less likely than in Rhodesia to have any decisive political effect.

On arrival I consulted Ton Vosloo, chairman of the main chain of Afrikaans-language newspapers. I explained that I was more anxious that any statements I made should be carried by the Afrikaans press, especially *Die Burger* in Cape Town and *Beeld* in Johannesburg, than in the English-language papers, who might be disposed to carry them anyway. Ton Vosloo reacted positively, though he advised me to make some gesture to the Afrikaners. This I tried to do, despite my imperfect knowledge of the language, by making part of my presentation of credentials speech in Afrikaans. It duly was carried on the state-controlled television.

In this, my first encounter with P.W. Botha, I pointed out that the Commonwealth heads of government would be meeting in Vancouver in October. Mrs Thatcher again would be under pressure to agree to additional sanctions. If there were further South African raids into the neighbouring countries, of the kind which had torpedoed the Commonwealth mission, those pressures would become irresistible. I added that I did not know whether I would see the end of apartheid during my time in South Africa, but I certainly hoped to contribute to a solution of the Namibia problem, which surely would be in South Africa's interests.

Like Mrs Thatcher, neither I nor anyone else I knew warmed to P.W. Botha on this or any other occasion. His domed head and tinted glasses gave him a sinister appearance. He was in the habit of receiving me in a study lit only by his desk lamp, conjuring up images of what it must have been like calling on Hitler in his bunker. He was prone to furious rages, and his Ministers were terrified of him. Shortly before I arrived in South Africa, P.W. Botha had released the hidden tape-recording of his meeting with a courageous political opponent, Van Zyl Slabbert, revealing that Slabbert, to be polite, had said one or two positive things about him and also had said that Chief Buthelezi, leader of Inkatha, wanted to be the only bull in the *kraal.* Enlightened by this experience, I made a silent vow before each of my encounters with P.W. Botha that it was not going to be to his advantage to publish the transcript of my meetings with him.

By this stage he had long since ceased to listen to the advice of anyone except his security chiefs. But this was to prove his undoing. His party no longer were consulted and, I discovered, many leading Afrikaners deeply resented what they regarded as his determination to turn the government of South Africa into a Latin American-style military *junta,* complete with death squads. This degree of resistance surprised and encouraged me as I had been assured in both London and Washington that the most likely successor to P.W. Botha was his chief henchman, General Magnus Malan.

Shortly after my call on Pik Botha, his deputy, Kobus Meiring, arranged for me to meet a dozen of the younger members of the National Party caucus. Several were to serve, subsequently, in the government of F.W. De Klerk and they were worried about the impasse in which South Africa found itself, internally and externally. Roelf Meyer, Leon Wessels, Sam de Beer and Renier Schoeman, as well as Meiring himself, were to turn out to be good friends over the next four years. The same could not be said for the Minister responsible

for negotiations, or rather the lack of them, Chris Heunis.
With a lugubrious walrus moustache, unmatchable pompos-
ity and a visceral hatred of the British, he made clear that
no interference by Mrs Thatcher in South Africa's affairs
would be tolerated. Fatally weakened in his constituency of
Stellenbosch by the challenge of Denis Worrall, formerly
the South African Ambassador in London, and cordially
detested by De Klerk, Heunis in the end resigned, replaced
by the courteous and scholarly Gerrit Viljoen.

General Malan also wanted nothing to do with the British,
but the Finance Minister, Barend du Plessis, and the future
National Party leader in the Cape, Dawie de Villiers, over
time became good friends. The Justice Minister, Kobie Coetsee,
also was a decent man, who had first humanized and then
liberalized the conditions of Mandela's imprisonment.

These, however, were not the most interesting of my first
encounters. So long as I had taken an interest in South
African affairs – an interest which began at Cambridge, where
earnest undergraduates sought to establish their anti-apartheid credentials by refusing to drink South African sherry –
the activities of Helen Suzman had always seemed to me to
offer the clearest beacon of hope that some kind of sanity
might in the end prevail.

When, nearly thirty years later, I arrived in South Africa
as a fledgling British Ambassador, I still had never met this
lady I so much admired. I did so with some trepidation. In
the course of her political career Helen Suzman had seen a
great many Ambassadors come and go – some, I was sure,
more memorable than others. Yet I was greeted with all the
warmth and helpfulness that had been shown to every one
of my predecessors and the innumerable other well-inten-
tioned foreigners who had regarded Helen as their most
reliable guide to the political labyrinth of apartheid. It took
me no time at all to discover that in addition to being the
most determined and effective opponent of injustice, Helen
was and is the most entertaining company it is possible to
find in South Africa – or elsewhere. However grim the circumstances, lunch with Helen was sure to end in gales of

laughter and I will never again be able to watch soda being poured into a glass of whisky without hearing Helen say: 'Don't drown it!'

She had campaigned relentlessly, for 13 years on her own in the South African Parliament, against every manifestation of apartheid – against grand apartheid and petty apartheid, forced removals and the homelands policy, detention without trial and all the innumerable other abuses of authority. She had campaigned against Dr Verwoerd's legislation banning the African National Congress, against the sentencing of Nelson Mandela and his associates to life imprisonment, against the utter inhumanity of the regime. And as Breyten Breytenbach, himself a prisoner, wrote, she had become Our Lady of the Prisoners. The *boere*, as he put it, 'didn't like her very much. They detested her sharp eye and her sharp tongue and her fearless criticism of whatever wrongs she saw.'* One of the prisoners she befriended, whose treatment she succeeded in getting improved and for whom she campaigned relentlessly, was Nelson Mandela.

He has never forgotten the debt he owes her. But this, at the time, did not help Helen with the anti-apartheid movements in Britain or the United States. For she had committed the heresy of questioning the wisdom of sanctions, the effect of which was to deprive large numbers of black South Africans of their jobs, and in particular of disinvestment. She also opposed measures which penalized the liberal English-speaking universities, while leaving the Afrikaans institutions largely unscathed. 'Those who support the cultural boycott', she declared, 'think they are on the side of the angels. In fact they are on the side of the idiots.' The last thing South African society needed, she believed, was further turning in on itself. What it required, in her view, was opening up to the outside world. We were returning from our first lunch together when, as we entered the parliamentary precinct, an Afrikaner guard peered into the car. Recognizing Helen and then me, he backed away. 'Can't you see the balloon coming out of his head? Conspiring with the enemy', Helen laughed.

* Breyten Breytenbach, *Confessions of an Albino Terrorist* (London: Faber and Faber, 1984), pp. 203–4.

My other first encounter which proved of real importance was with F.W. De Klerk. The reports were not encouraging. As befitted the leader of the National Party in the Transvaal, he was said to be deeply conservative. As Minister of Education, he had been charged by P.W. Botha with further muzzling the universities. My own impressions were rather different. For De Klerk, noting my role in Rhodesia, said that he wanted me to know that if he had his way, South Africa would not make the same mistake. What, I enquired, did he think the mistake had been? 'Leaving it much too late to negotiate with the real black leaders', De Klerk replied.

In Pretoria and Johannesburg, I met three other Afrikaners who became both friends and powerful allies. The first of these was Pieter de Lange, head of the secret society which linked together the Afrikaner elite – the *Broederbond*. For decades this had been regarded by outsiders as exerting a most sinister influence. And it was true that the *Broederbond* was dedicated to the promotion of Afrikaner interests and, above all, culture and was one of the mainstays of the regime. Pieter de Lange, however, had circulated to the members of this society a most remarkable discussion document, in which he invited them to think the unthinkable. Suppose, it said, there was an African majority in Parliament and in the government one day, how then could Afrikaner interests be protected? Warning clearly of the impossibility of preserving the *status quo*, the document contained the striking phrase: 'the greatest risk is not taking any risks'.

No less impressive than De Lange was the head of the Dutch Reformed Church, Professor Johan Heyns. I spent many hours with him at his modest bungalow in a suburb of Pretoria. Professor Heyns had declared apartheid a heresy, thereby splitting his church and provoking the fury of the conservatives. In many tight corners over the next four years, he was to prove the most influential of friends.

The Governor of the Reserve Bank, Gerhard de Kock, was one of the most respected of the world's central bankers. The 1985 debt standstill he saw as an utter disaster. It meant that South Africa, a developing country, could no longer import capital to help meet the demands of its people. Instead, South African savings had to be exported to reduce the debt. This meant running a large trade surplus and curtailing growth to 2 per cent or less per annum to avoid sucking in imports. De Kock understood that, in the end, this haemorrhage was bound to be fatal, with the South African population increasing by a million people a year and close to half the urban black population unemployed. This the security chiefs were simply unable to grasp. At a meeting with them, De Kock told me in amazement, they had explained that all that was required was to imprison a few thousand more agitators and South Africa's problems would be solved.

The views of these influential Afrikaners were little known to the outside world, but there was another Afrikaner whose activities were making the headlines. Two years before, Van Zyl Slabbert had suddenly resigned as head of the Progressive Federal Party and given up his parliamentary seat, to the fury of his colleagues, including Helen Suzman. This he did because he believed that the Parliament was increasingly irrelevant. Slabbert proceeded instead to arrange a meeting in Senegal between a group of white South Africans, mainly dissident Afrikaners, and the ANC. This produced a furious reaction from P.W. Botha who, quoting Lenin, denounced Slabbert and his friends as 'useful idiots'. In an effort to help protect Slabbert, as he returned to Cape Town amidst threats to assassinate him, we and other embassies organized a reception party at the airport. P.W. Botha was making clear that he had no intention of negotiating, then or later, with the ANC.

14 Repression

When I arrived in South Africa, relations with the leaders of the United Democratic Front were strained because of the British government's opposition to further sanctions. I explained to Archbishop Tutu that we would continue to disagree about disinvestment, because I genuinely believed that many of those who disinvested were unlikely to return, but that he would find us determined and, I hoped, effective allies in the struggle against apartheid.

Many of the British companies operating in South Africa, including BP, Shell, Unilever and RTZ, had set outstanding examples in terms of pensions, health, welfare, housing and other programmes they provided for their employees. To the more than 200 British companies active in South Africa, I made clear that we hoped they would stay. But if they did, they would need to have an impeccable record in terms of the opportunities and support they provided for their non-white employees. In all but a handful of cases, they did stay; and in all but one or two cases, they did a great deal to undermine apartheid through their programmes.

It was obvious, however, that much greater efforts needed to be made to establish relationships with the future leadership of the country. This was far from easy, as most of them were in exile or in jail. Two or three of the younger members of the Embassy and Consulates had good contacts in the townships. I encouraged them to abandon all other work and concentrate exclusively on developing those relationships. It was difficult and sometimes dangerous but very rewarding work, and they did it to such effect that they became known as the township attachés.

It was not possible to send young members of the Embassy into the townships, still less to visit them myself, as I aimed most weeks to do, without doing more to help the people in them. First Chris Patten and then Lynda Chalker, as the Ministers in charge of overseas aid, allocated the relatively modest sums needed to enable us to support, eventually, over three hundred small projects in Soweto, Mamelodi,

Crossroads, Guguletu and many of the other townships and squatter camps in the Cape and the Transvaal.

These projects, amazingly, were controversial at the time as it was argued, mainly outside South Africa, that this was merely ameliorating apartheid and, therefore, postponing the day of reckoning. Given my experience of conditions elsewhere in Africa, this doctrine of 'worse is better' did not appeal. Above all it did not appeal to people in the townships, who desperately needed help and support. Virtually all the projects we supported were run by determined opponents of the regime and when their party was unbanned we discovered what we knew already – that we had established contact with most of the local leadership of the ANC.

I tried also to establish friendships with a number of ex-Robben Islanders who had served long sentences in prison with Mandela. Several of those who had been released belonged to the Africanist tradition, including Neville Alexander and Fikhile Bam, who had helped to make the film *Robben Island – Our University*. Dikgang Moseneke also belonged to this group. In Soweto, Dr Ntatho Motlana continued to play a prominent role on behalf of the ANC. I also tried to show all the support I could for the Delmas treason triallists, Popo Molefe and Terror Lekota, and that support was rewarded by their friendship when they emerged from jail.

In Johannesburg I made contact with Cyril Ramaphosa, leader of the National Union of Mineworkers, at the time in the thick of a miners' strike. Ramaphosa, an exceptionally skilful negotiator, assured me that he had no intention of 'doing a Scargill' and destroying his own union. One week later, the strike was settled.

While these efforts were being made to expand our contacts with the black leadership, in November 1987 Margaret Thatcher attended the Commonwealth Conference in Vancouver. She went there determined to yield no further ground on sanctions. She pointed out that most of the neighbouring countries were dependent on the South African economy. At a press conference she was confronted with a statement by an ANC spokesman that, in view of her attitude, British companies in South Africa would become legitimate targets for attack. Mrs Thatcher exploded, declaring that this showed what a typical terrorist organization the ANC was. The UDF declared a boycott of all contact with British government representatives.

I was not very worried about the UDF boycott as we had established such a wide range of contacts that I expected few, if any, of them to be interrupted. But I was concerned that 10 Downing Street should understand that I had to go on dealing with the leaders of the internal wing of the ANC and we must maintain our well-established contacts with them in Lusaka. This was accepted.

In February 1988, P.W. Botha attempted to suppress what resistance remained by banning the UDF. Most of its leaders were already in detention but, evidently, he did not feel that was enough. As I met a group of National Party MPs on the steps of Parliament, I asked about their reaction to the news. They looked at me in amazement. None of them had been informed, let alone consulted. The decision had been taken by the President and his security chiefs alone.

The church leaders organized a meeting in Cape Town Cathedral, to be followed by a march on Parliament. I sent members of my Embassy to witness the demonstration. The church leaders explained that if stopped by the police, the demonstrators should kneel on the pavement and start singing a hymn. With these instructions, they set off.

As they rounded the corner towards the Parliament building, the demonstrators ran into the South African riot police, led by the redoubtable Major Dolf Odendal. Archbishop Tutu and Allan Boesak fell to their knees, as did the congregation. Unimpressed, Odendal opened up with water cannon filled with purple dye; following which he arrested Tutu and Boesak, the wife of the Canadian Ambassador and the BBC crew filming the incident.

They were quickly released and by lunch time Allan Boesak, never a one for martyrdom, was to be found eating a lobster in the Tuynhuis restaurant nearby. Meanwhile I was deluged with calls from London, including Lambeth Palace, urging me to secure the release of him and Desmond Tutu. That evening, I had dinner with F.W. De Klerk at the Mount Nelson hotel. One of the 'liberal' English-speaking businessmen present did not distinguish himself that evening but Johann Rupert, son of Anton Rupert, the great Afrikaner businessman and philanthropist, did. He had been visiting Taiwan, he said, to finalize a large investment in South Africa when, on turning on his television, he had discovered the Minister of Law and Order stating that the country was on the verge of revolution and that, therefore, the UDF must be banned. Johann Rupert, who had himself been threatened by General Malan, told De Klerk what would happen to the country and its economy if the security *junta* who were now running it continued to perform in this way. I described in detail what had happened at the demonstration we had witnessed earlier in the day. De Klerk made very clear, with surprising frankness, that he had not been consulted and that if he had been in charge, affairs would have been conducted in a very different way.

At the end of the parliamentary session, I was invited to address the annual meeting in Johannesburg of the Urban Foundation. It was an opportunity to deliver a decidedly undiplomatic speech. In the 1960s, I pointed out, South Africa had been able to maintain apartheid and still have economic growth. That was not possible any longer. South Africa was approaching a further turning-point in its relations with the outside world. 'We do not believe in your isolation; but we cannot prevent you isolating yourselves. . . . If you want to get out of a hole, the first thing to do is to stop digging.' Unless South Africa scrapped the remaining apartheid laws, they would get no continuing support from us.

This was extensively reported in the Afrikaans press. There was a lot of support from the Johannesburg business community, increasingly alarmed at P.W. Botha's disregard for the economic consequences of his actions. With Harry Oppenheimer and other business leaders, we attempted to work out a loan guarantee scheme to try to increase the availability of low-cost housing, desperately needed to help cope with the flood of people moving from the countryside into ever-worsening shanty towns on the outskirts of all the major cities. This was no easy task given, among other problems, the prevalence of rent boycotts which, for obvious reasons, were an exceptionally popular form of protest.

With some very distinguished exceptions, most members of the business community were chary of any direct involvement in politics. Many had remained silent throughout the apartheid era and those who publicly criticized the regime frequently had suffered ostracism for their pains. Yet many South African business leaders had contributed to the erosion of apartheid through their support for social programmes and through the way they managed their enterprises. At this stage, and hardly surprisingly, few believed that they might see an ANC-led government in power within a few years. But the balance within the business world had shifted towards those who were convinced that things could not go on as they were; and nothing was more certain than that a future majority government was going to need their support.

My other main task in this period was to try to save the lives of the Sharpeville Six, condemned to death for the murder of a black town councillor. About one of the Six I had very mixed feelings, as he was directly responsible for the man's death. But certainly for the others, the penalty was excessive and if carried out would have been certain to trigger a further wave of violence. Given the character of P.W. Botha, it was going to be no easy task to get them off Death Row.

I was able, however, to find some redoubtable allies. I appealed to Professor Heyns who suggested that we should each aim to see President Botha – separately, but on the same day. It would not be easy, even for P.W. Botha, to disregard the views of the head of the Dutch Reformed Church.

The other important ally was Helen Suzman. Except across the floor in Parliament, Helen had refused to speak to P.W. Botha for more than 20 years. For when, in 1966, Hendrik Verwoerd was stabbed to death in the Parliament Chamber, P.W. Botha, arms flailing and eyes bulging, had rushed across the floor to shout at her: 'It's you who did this. It's all you liberals ... we will get the lot of you.' Helen insisted on an apology and for the next 30 years cut off all further contact with him – save for the withering attacks she made on him in Parliament.

Now she felt that the situation that would face South Africa if the Sharpeville Six were executed was so serious that she must go to see P.W. Botha with her friend and the leader of her party, Colin Eglin. They reminded him that his mentor, Dr D.F. Malan, had pleaded successfully for the lives of two Afrikaner Nazi sympathizers, who had placed a bomb in a post office during the Second World War.

At the eleventh hour, a reprieve was granted. Several of P.W. Botha's Ministers expressed to me their relief that our concerted efforts had worked.

There were other ways in which we tried to show our support for those genuinely combating apartheid. When the *Weekly Mail*, which was playing an invaluable role in exposing the abuses of the security forces, was suspended by the authorities, we helped to tide it over until it could resume publication.

Most of the homeland leaders were creatures of the regime. But this was not the case of Enos Mabuza in Kangwane, who was coping heroically with a flood of Mozambican refugees and for his pains was being harassed by the security police. A combination of practical help for the refugees and well-publicized visits to Kangwane helped to earn him some respite. For this, I received a message of thanks from the ANC in Lusaka.

At about this time, Wim Wepener, editor of *Beeld*, the main Afrikaans newspaper in the Transvaal, came to see me, to request an interview with Mrs Thatcher. Wepener was no liberal, but *Beeld* was starting to take a more independent line *vis-à-vis* the government and increasingly to represent *verligte* ('enlightened') Afrikaner thinking. I was able to persuade Mrs Thatcher to see Wepener and encouraged him to ask the question: what is the difference between the ANC and the IRA? I was then consulted about the reply. *Beeld* duly appeared with a banner headline: 'The IRA have the vote and the ANC do not'.

This made a considerable impression at the time. When in a speech, I pressed again for the release of Mandela and other prisoners, *Beeld* published an editorial calling for the release of Mandela. This produced a furious reaction from P.W. Botha who, addressing the Natal Congress of his party, said that it was the duty of the Afrikaans press to support the National Party. This in turn produced an amazing editorial from Wepener, sticking to his guns on the release of Mandela, and concluding: 'We are not the South African Broadcasting Corporation – at any rate, not yet!' The SABC, notorious for its servility to the government, carried an early morning 'commentary' in unctuous tones eerily reminiscent of Lord Haw-Haw. P.W. Botha on one occasion flew into a ferocious rage over the evening television news, telephoned the producer and had the news changed before the end of the programme!

South Africa was blessed with a number of remarkable editors, the most courageous of all being Aggrey Klaaste, editor of the *Sowetan* – the most widely read newspaper. Aggrey, who belonged to the 'Africanist' tradition, was not a member of the ANC. He was just as fearless a critic of school boycotts and of the senseless slogan 'liberation before education' as he was of the misdeeds of the regime. He too sought and got an interview with Mrs Thatcher, printing her denunciation of the apartheid laws alongside her arguments against inflicting further economic punishment on South Africa.

While, by this time, many had given up on any prospect for negotiations, I knew from those who had been imprisoned with him that Nelson Mandela believed in the absolute necessity of discussions between the government and the ANC. In a memorandum, top secret at the time, addressed to P.W. Botha, Mandela noted the need to reconcile the demand for majority rule in a unitary state with the concern that majority rule would not mean black domination and oppression of the white minority.

Within the liberation movement, there were doubts even about Mandela's strategy. For it was part of the conventional wisdom at the time that if the ANC were perceived as too 'moderate', it would be supplanted by more extreme parties, notably the Pan African Congress (PAC) with its slogan 'one settler, one bullet' (particularly mindless when it was in fact the settlers who had the bullets) and the Azanian

People's Organization (AZAPO). I was very sceptical of such claims, being unimpressed by the leadership or organizing ability of the PAC and disconcerted to be told by my friend Jerry Mosala, head of AZAPO, that he intended to leave the country for three years to take up a chair in contextual theology at Cambridge! From our contacts in the townships I had no doubt of the strength of the still partly subterranean ANC organization or of the authority Mandela could command if it ever became possible to secure his release.

15 Namibia

As I had told P.W. Botha, I went to South Africa not knowing how much contribution I might be able to make to the ending of apartheid, but determined to combine my efforts with those of my friend Dr Chester Crocker, Assistant Secretary for Africa under President Reagan, to secure a resolution of the Namibia problem. That at least, I was convinced, ought to be attainable. Crocker had been criticized for linking South African withdrawal from Namibia to the withdrawal of the 30 000 Cuban troops in Angola. Personally I believed that linkage was justified, both because it was in any event desirable to get the Cubans out of Angola and because I did not see how, otherwise, we were going to persuade the South Africans to withdraw from Namibia.

In October 1987 the MPLA government in Angola, led by President Dos Santos, launched its great offensive designed finally to crush Savimbi's UNITA guerrillas in their main redoubt in south-eastern Angola. The offensive, which involved the movement of tens of thousands of men, was meticulously planned by the Angolan army's Soviet military advisers. As the massive force they assembled advanced south and east from the provincial capital of Cuito Cuanavale towards Savimbi's headquarters at Jamba, they were ambushed on the Lomba river. The leading brigade was decimated. The rest of the force withdrew in confusion to Cuito Cuanavale, suffering further losses as it did so. Savimbi claimed a great victory.

In fact the victory was won by a remarkably small but militarily effective contingent of South African forces. The South Africans had been operating in Angola ever since 1975, when Henry Kissinger encouraged them to intervene to prevent the Communist-backed MPLA seizing the capital, Luanda. When that venture failed, the main South African forces withdrew.

Having fallen back to the Namibian border, they soon discovered that the most effective way to disrupt infiltration by the South West African People's Organization (SWAPO) into northern Namibia was by intercepting them in southern

Angola. This was done through the use of small but determined special forces, South African-led, but with Bushmen
trackers. Angolan opponents of the regime in Luanda were
organized into the Portuguese-speaking 32 Battalion, which
specialized in cross-border operations. At the same time the
South African Defence Force continued the supply of
weaponry and fuel to Savimbi's UNITA guerrillas and sought
to co-ordinate military operations with them. As necessary,
these were supported by South African units. By these tactics,
over the next 14 years the South Africans turned much of
southern Angola into a free-fire zone.

The South African Foreign Ministry continued to issue
strenuous denials that South Africa was in any way involved
in the fighting in Angola. Nor did Colonel Jan Breytenbach
and his colleagues on the border very often bother to seek
political approval for their operations. These received the
support they required from the South African military command. As P.W. Botha and his colleagues became frequent
visitors to Savimbi's South African-supplied headquarters in
Jamba, they knew perfectly well the extent of these cross-
border incursions.

Stopping the massive Soviet- and Cuban-backed advance
in October 1987 required some quite heroic actions by 32
Battalion and the other heavily outnumbered South African forces involved. The South African force never exceeded
a brigade in size. The battle was won by concentrated artillery fire and air-strikes on the Angolan tank formations. Huge
quantities of Soviet equipment were destroyed or captured.
As always, the public credit for the victory was awarded to
UNITA, despite Colonel Breytenbach's low regard for their
fighting qualities. The Soviet military advisers took an even
dimmer view of the performance of their Angolan allies.

Visiting Namibia at the end of the year, I was briefed by
a half-mad South African Colonel on the battle of the Lomba
river, which was indeed a most impressive military exploit.
On the struggle against SWAPO in Namibia, he took the
view that victory was certain – but for the efforts of the enemy
within. When I enquired who the enemy within were, he
replied: 'The churches, the trade unions and the teachers.'

After their victory on the Lomba river, the South African
forces still operating hundreds of kilometres inside Angola

overreached themselves. It never was the intention of General Jannie Geldenhuys, head of the South African Defence Force, that they should try to take and hold Cuito Cuanavale. As, however, they attempted to eliminate the Angolan bridgehead on the east bank of the Cuito river, they found themselves up against Cuban armour and heavy artillery fire. The South African attempt to eliminate the bridgehead was beaten off.

Stung by the failure of their great offensive, the Cuban commanders now decided on an effective military response. Hitherto, they had kept their forces well back from the Namibian border and away from South African attacks on infiltrating SWAPO. Cuban forces in the western sector now were reinforced and instructed to move south of Menongue and Lubango in Cunene province, bringing them much closer to the border. Their tank formations posed a serious threat to the lightly armed South African reconnaissance forces, hitherto used to operating with impunity in the area. The South Africans had to wonder whether the Cuban tanks might seek to cross the border, where there was not enough South African armour to oppose them. For both sides the war had entered a new and potentially much more dangerous phase, with the possibility of a direct South African/Cuban confrontation.

In international affairs, some problems are easier to tackle when they have reached the point of crisis than when they are merely heading there. While acknowledging the skill their forces had shown in the battle on the Lomba river, I asked the South Africans whether they did not think they were in danger of overreaching themselves. My friend Professor Johan Heyns enquired publicly whether it made sense to have young men 'defending South Africa' 200 miles inside Angola. The South Africans had suffered significant casualties and theirs was a citizen army. Several of those killed were conscripts. Attending a dinner in Johannesburg at the house of a National Party MP, I found that virtually everyone there agreed with Professor Heyns – including the MP. The sole military representative present was hard put to it to justify himself.

South Africa was fortunate at this juncture in having a most remarkable public servant, Neil Van Heerden, at the head of its Foreign Ministry. We spent countless hours together discussing ways to breathe fresh life into the Namibia negotiations. The South Africans hitherto had never really been prepared to contemplate giving up Namibia. Now that the stakes had risen, I argued, it was in their interests to consider doing so – provided agreement could be reached on a credible programme for Cuban withdrawal from Angola.

For the United States, Crocker was continuing indefatigably to work that side of the problem and he too was beginning to sense a breakthrough. For the war in Angola was increasingly unpopular in Cuba. The Russians, increasingly disillusioned, were beginning to contemplate cutting their losses in Africa. There was suddenly opening up the potential for movement.

In January 1988 the Angolans for the first time indicated a willingness to agree in principle to eventual total Cuban withdrawal. This was to be phased over four years. The South Africans remained deeply sceptical. In May, we made available a venue in London for the first in a new series of consultations, led by Crocker, between the South Africans, Cubans and Angolans. In June the discussions resumed in Cairo, this time with Pik Botha and General Malan leading the South African delegation – and conducting some well-publicized tourism on camels by the pyramids.

Further meetings followed at various venues. Our involvement was indirect but important. For the Americans had no embassy in Luanda. We served as the indispensable channel of communication for them there, and often were able to influence the Angolan replies. Following the imposition by Congress of general sanctions against South Africa, there had been a virtual breakdown of relations between the US Administration and the South African government. So we had to do a good deal of the heavy lifting in Pretoria, not only with Pik Botha and Van Heerden, but with other members of the South African government.

By the middle of the year Van Heerden was telling me that there had been a sea-change in the South African attitude. This was because the political leadership felt that the military had indeed overreached themselves and further casualties were unacceptable around Cuito Cuanavale. The South Africans also had begun to realize that a profound change really was taking place in Soviet policy.

South African, and possibly also Cuban, minds were concentrated by incidents on the battlefield on 26–27 June 1988. As Cuban forces were now close up against the Namibian border near the Calueque hydroelectric power station on the Cunene river, the South Africans engaged a Cuban column north of the border, inflicting a good many casualties. In retaliation Cuban MiGs bombed the dam and the pumping-station which, though it had for years been controlled by the South Africans, was on the Angolan side of the river. The dam and pumping-station were damaged and 11 South Africans were killed. These were the first major direct clashes between Cuban and South African forces. Having tasted blood, some of it their own, both sides drew back from further exploits of this kind.

Van Heerden and Pik Botha, from the beginning of this round of negotiations, had been working hard for a settlement. To convince P.W. Botha and the South African military, they needed to be able to persuade them that Cuban withdrawal really was assured. At a meeting in New York in mid-July the new leader of the Cuban delegation, Carlos Aldana, told Van Heerden that they were interested in a 'peace without losers'. Going further than any European Foreign Ministry was prepared to do at the time, Aldana added that linkage (of Namibian independence to Cuban troop withdrawal) 'exists and its existence is accepted'. One month later, in Geneva, Van Heerden responded by proposing that the process leading to Namibian independence should be started – once the South Africans were satisfied about the modalities for Cuban withdrawal. By October the two sides were arguing about whether that withdrawal should be phased over two or two-and-a-half years.

By this stage I was convinced that a Namibia settlement was within our grasp. Neither South Africa nor Cuba had any real desire any longer to bear the escalating costs of the war. By November a schedule had been worked out whereby Cuban forces in southern Angola would withdraw to the north – and then leave. On 22 December, this agreement was signed in New York – a triumph of persistence for Chet Crocker and his team.

But Crocker by now was close to leaving the scene, both of his own volition and because the new US Secretary of State, James Baker, seemed to feel that he had become too much of a liability with Congress. As my experience in Rhodesia led me to suspect that implementing the settlement would be no less difficult than negotiating it, I was dismayed by this news. Crocker made clear to me that we were going to have to take on much of the burden of helping to ensure that it was in fact implemented.

Mrs Thatcher was due to make a visit at the end of March 1989 to Nigeria, Zimbabwe and Malawi. I wanted her to end this tour in Namibia, arriving there on 1 April – the day on which the UN plan, to which the South Africans now had agreed, began to be implemented. But we would not know until the last moment what the situation would be in the Namibian capital, Windhoek, on that day. I went ahead to Windhoek and it was agreed by Mrs Thatcher that a decision should be taken only as she was about to leave Malawi.

Having talked to the South African Administrator, the UN Representatives, Marti Ahtisaari and General Prem Chand, the British Signals contingent providing communications for the UN force and a number of black Namibian friends, I sent a message urging her to come. There was plenty of opposing advice at the time, but come she did.

So as Namibia returned to legality, the Prime Ministerial VC10 arrived at Windhoek airport. Mrs Thatcher had lunch in their tented camp with the British military contingent. We then set off for the British-owned Rossing uranium mine, on which Namibia depended for a third of its exports. There had been many pressures on RTZ to close down the mine, which would have been a disaster for Namibia, as key markets would have been lost and it would have been extremely difficult ever to open it up again. Instead it had set an example to the rest of Namibia by developing housing, health, pensions, safety and other standards far above those I had seen anywhere else in Africa.

As we boarded the plane for Rossing, the first reports were coming in of large-scale SWAPO incursions and clashes on the Angolan border. By the time we returned to Windhoek, it was clear that a crisis had developed of a magnitude that threatened the entire settlement.

The South African Administrator, Louis Pienaar, reported that large armed SWAPO columns crossing the border, contrary to the terms of the cease-fire agreement, had been intercepted by the South African forces. This was exactly the situation we had faced in Rhodesia when, immediately following the cease-fire, large numbers of Mugabe's guerrilla forces moved across the Mozambique border into Rhodesia with their weapons. It had been touch-and-go to dissuade the Rhodesians from attacking them. In this case, we were dealing with the South Africans, with much more formidable military capabilities. Both sides were already behaving as if the agreement was no longer in existence. Marti Ahtisaari, who had joined us at Pienaar's residence, was in an impossibly difficult position. It was clear that the South Africans were on the verge of withdrawing from the settlement. Mrs Thatcher told Ahtisaari that he must get agreement from the UN Secretary-General to authorize South African ground forces to stop the SWAPO incursions.

The scene shifted to a long and extremely difficult meeting with Pik Botha at the airport. Under pressure from P.W. Botha, he was adamant that the South Africans would have to take the law into their own hands and call in air-strikes against the SWAPO columns whether the UN authorized these or not. Mrs Thatcher said that she had told Ahtisaari that he must call Pérez de Cuéllar and get him to authorize the local South African forces to deal with these incursions, but that if the South Africans took unilateral action, 'the whole world will be against you – led by me!'

I argued strongly against air-strikes. This went on for two hours, until Denis Thatcher mercifully intervened, as the Prime Minister had to get her plane. As I returned to Windhoek, I was told that the UN had authorized action to deal with the incursions and Pik Botha told me the air-strikes had been called off. Margaret Thatcher boarded her plane extremely reluctantly. She clearly was attracted by the prospect of continuing to conduct the affairs of Namibia. Marti Ahtisaari was heavily criticized for his actions and had to show real political courage in taking them. If he had not done so, the settlement would have been lost.*

* Marti Ahtisaari became President of Finland in 1994.

But it remained to control the military situation. Unlike the Americans and the South Africans, we had an Embassy in Luanda where our excellent Ambassador, James Glaze, was in direct touch with the Angolan Chief of Staff. Neither he, the Cubans nor the Russians wanted the SWAPO incursions to continue: they realized what was at stake. So did several of the senior members of the SWAPO political leadership, also contacted by Glaze. Gradually the situation was brought back under control, but not before several hundred SWAPO guerrillas had been killed.

Ahtisaari and Prem Chand continued to experience difficulties with the South African government, requiring frequent interventions by us, over the return of SWAPO leaders and refugees. When the SWAPO leaders did return to Windhoek, I invited Hage Geingob (who became Prime Minister on Namibia's independence), Theo Ben Gurirab (Foreign Minister) and Hamutenya (Minister of Trade) to lunch at the Kalahari Sands hotel. We had kept in touch with them throughout their years of exile. I explained that I did not expect them to feel any particular affinity with a Conservative government in Britain – or vice versa. We did not agree with their quasi-Marxist economic views and hoped that they would change them. But we were determined to see that they were given a fair chance in free elections and I expected them to win. If they did, we would help the new government to get established, just as we had in Zimbabwe and elsewhere.

The response was very positive. The SWAPO leaders made clear that they were determined to preserve the Namibian economy. I encouraged them to visit Rossing, which they did shortly afterwards and were as impressed as I had been by what they found there.

Not long afterwards the leading white member of SWAPO, Anton Lubowski, was assassinated. I had got to know him quite well and had no doubt that this exploit was the work of undeclared elements of South African intelligence. It was a black day when I attended his funeral in the township, where Theo Ben Gurirab made an emotional appeal for calm.

As the elections, due in November, drew closer I also had no doubt that we would witness a final attempt by South African military intelligence to disrupt them. What could not be predicted was what form this would take.

One day in Pretoria I was suddenly summoned, with the other Western Ambassadors, to an urgent meeting with Pik Botha and General Geldenhuys. Pik Botha read out intercepted radio messages which purported to show that another massive SWAPO incursion was planned, with the connivance of the Kenyan battalion of the UN force. As we controlled the UN's communications in Namibia, it took me about three hours to discover, and not much longer to warn Van Heerden, that these messages were false. A furious Pik Botha had been misled by his own intelligence services. The crisis passed, SWAPO winning the elections by a large margin.

On 20 March 1990, I attended the celebrations in Windhoek of Namibia's independence. It was a chaotic evening, with Pérez de Cuéllar and various heads of state barely able to get into the stadium and Yasser Arafat attempting to accost James Baker, who was by no means anxious to meet him at the time. But there also was no doubting the sense of joy, and also of relief, among the immense crowd gathered there at the attainment of self-rule and the end of a long and bitter conflict.

16 De Klerk

In January 1989, P.W. Botha suffered a stroke while preparing for the state opening of Parliament. Very unwisely from his point of view, he invited the National Party to elect a new leader in Parliament, though he had no intention of standing down as President. It was clear that the succession would be decided between two politicians – F.W. De Klerk and the Finance Minister, Barend du Plessis – with whom I had very friendly relations. General Magnus Malan, whom so many foreign observers had regarded as a likely successor, to my certain knowledge had just one vote in the parliamentary caucus – his own.

Barend du Plessis was supported by many, though not all, of the *verligte* National Party MPs. He also was believed to be the favoured choice of P.W. Botha – not because the 'old crocodile' suddenly had reverted to being a reformist but, I suspect, because he believed that Barend would have less of an independent power base than De Klerk. The result, in a vote of the National Party MPs, was a relatively narrow victory for De Klerk.

With P.W. Botha still incapacitated, De Klerk followed up his victory by making a decidedly reformist speech. There were some who believed this still to be play-acting. His brother, Wimpie, told me in dismay that De Klerk was far too conservative to be a good President. I said that he knew his brother better than I did, but my impression was different.

A couple of days after his election I went to see De Klerk on his own, in his small office in Parliament. I told him that if he was able to take South Africa in a different direction, we would try to help him. I added that if the security police and military intelligence were allowed to continue their activities unchecked, there was no way any of us were going to be able to help South Africa. We had evidence that, despite all the disclaimers, South African military intelligence were continuing actively to support RENAMO in Mozambique.

There followed a long battle of wills between P.W. Botha,

slowly recovering, and the man he inadvertently had designated as his successor. I was convinced that P.W. Botha would lose this battle, as the relief among National Party MPs when De Klerk took over the leadership of the party was palpable. Suddenly, they all counted for something again and the security chiefs no longer had an absolutely predominant role.

It became possible to discuss with members of the government a whole range of issues that were forbidden territory so long as they were terrified of their master. It was also possible to establish a regular pattern of meetings with De Klerk, who increasingly had convinced us of his intention to make major changes. De Klerk's friends were not the security chiefs, but the business community of Johannesburg, and precisely those leading Afrikaners who had felt alienated under P.W. Botha.

Gerhard de Kock, Governor of the Reserve Bank, by this time was dying of cancer. He was a golf-playing friend of De Klerk, and I urged him to explain to the new leader of the National Party what would happen to South Africa, with the population increasing by a million people a year, if the capital outflow continued. De Kock needed no persuasion. He spent the last months of his life convincing his friend that only disaster could result from continuance on the existing course.

In May, I arranged for De Klerk to visit Mrs Thatcher at Chequers. At the time this was still an unpopular thing to do: we were accused of colluding with the apartheid regime. In fact Mrs Thatcher made clear to De Klerk, with her customary lack of ambiguity, the necessity of proceeding with the Namibia settlement and of releasing Mandela. She found De Klerk openminded and a refreshing contrast to P.W. Botha, but remained uncertain how far he would be prepared to go.

In an attempt to show that he could still play an independent role, P.W. Botha summoned Nelson Mandela from prison to tea in his office. Mandela is generous about this meeting in his memoirs. To me, I am afraid, it appeared that President Botha was simply trying to use an encounter with the man he and his colleagues had kept imprisoned for 27 years to try to show that, politically, he was not dead yet.

As P.W. Botha attempted to cling on to power, in August

De Klerk and his senior colleagues made clear to him that he would have to resign as President and that they intended to call new elections. Shortly beforehand, I had called on P.W. Botha – not least to assure myself that he was not about to try to make a comeback. It was not the desire that was lacking but, by this time, he had lost all support in his party.

De Klerk called an election before taking over as President. In it he succeeded in beating off the challenge from the right-wing Conservative party led by Andries Treurnicht. As we assembled for the open-air ceremony at the Union Buildings in Pretoria at which De Klerk was to be sworn in as President, the Justice Minister, Kobie Coetsee, asked me if he was going to announce the release of Mandela. I said that I did not think so, as that would require preparation and De Klerk anyway was not the man to take great initiatives without consulting his Cabinet!

De Klerk's speech was very positive in tone, but non-specific. But his first act as President was to prohibit use of the *sjambok* – the whips the South African police had employed for decades as their favourite method of crowd control. He was faced immediately with a much bigger decision.

During the election campaign in the Cape, a number of coloured youths had been killed in violent clashes with the police. Archbishop Tutu and Allan Boesak called me and the other Western Ambassadors to the Archbishop's home at Bishopscourt to say that a large demonstration was being organized to coincide with the opening of Parliament. If it were not permitted to take place, they predicted further violence, with Allan Boesak as usual taking a more militant line than Desmond Tutu.

From the meeting at Bishopscourt, I went to see Pik Botha. He and Van Heerden needed no convincing that the demonstration should be authorized: otherwise De Klerk's Presidency would get off to the worst possible start. But the security chiefs were opposed.

As, next morning, I continued my lobbying of the South African government, Johan Heyns walked into my office, accompanied by half the leadership of the Dutch Reformed

Church. They had flown down from Pretoria and had heard that we were trying to get the demonstration authorized. I regarded this delegation as, quite literally, heaven-sent! They went off to see De Klerk, determined that he should not start his Presidency on the same footing as P.W. Botha. De Klerk agreed. I was asked to help get assurances from the church leaders that if the police stayed on the sidelines, they would help to guarantee that the demonstration was peaceful.

When it took place, we held our breaths as a large crowd assembled. The church and UDF leaders managed effectively to marshal the demonstration. The event passed off peacefully.

It was a turning-point in South Africa's history, as De Klerk proceeded to authorize numerous other demonstrations. He followed this by making a remarkable speech, in private, to most of the hierarchy of the South African police. The police, he said, for too long had been asked by South Africa's politicians to solve the country's political problems for them. He wanted the police in future to stick to their proper task, which was to combat crime and violence, while he sought to deal with the politics.

One of the first issues I had raised with De Klerk when he took over as leader had been the continuance of South African support for RENAMO. Orders were now given to terminate that support. This did not prevent elements of South African military intelligence continuing to help their friends across the border, but it did impede their efforts, which no longer enjoyed tacit support from the very top. The State Security Council were told that the politics of repression were getting South Africa nowhere. As De Klerk put it, they were trying to stamp out a bush-fire which then simply flared up elsewhere on the *veld.* These problems had to be tackled at their political source.

Yet despite this change of direction at the top, military intelligence and the security police went on acting as laws to themselves. This continued even when, in an effort to exert control, De Klerk abolished the security branch and merged them with the ordinary police. In order to be able to state publicly that South African Defence Force personnel were not involved in assassination attempts against ANC members or sympathizers at home and abroad, military intelligence had created the infamous 'Civil Co-operation Bureau' – a bunch of killers who continued to be financed from secret funds. The names of several of these agents were known, including that of Colonel Eugene de Kock, who commanded the unit at Vlakplaas which was responsible for numerous atrocities.

A source of constant irritation, though also some amusement, were the Fred Karno antics of the South African intelligence services. Determined to monitor our telephones, they did so in such inept ways that each move of the Embassy to Cape Town was followed by the appearance of a group of technicians whose interference with the junction box outside the Embassy gates invariably managed to put it out of action for several hours before it was reconnected and declared fit for us to use.

Their efforts were not always so benign. My friend Bob Frasure, political counsellor in the American Embassy, was engaged in monitoring the cross-border exploits of the South African Defence Force. As he discovered more about these than military intelligence wished him to know, they retaliated by terrorizing his wife and children during his absences from home, to such effect that Frasure had to be withdrawn.* Why the State Department permitted this to happen without publicizing the circumstances, I have never been able to understand.

We redoubled our efforts, meanwhile, to get South Africa to terminate its military nuclear programme, centred on the uranium separation plant at Velindaba. The Finance Minister, Barend du Plessis, was a powerful ally. He could not understand what use South Africa could possibly make of nuclear weapons – 'we can', as he observed, 'hardly drop them on Lusaka or Soweto' – and opposed any further resources being devoted to the programme. De Klerk, taking the same view, ordered the closure of the plan at Velindaba, thereby terminating any further development of the military nuclear programme. Orders subsequently were given by him to decommission the seven nuclear devices the South Africans already had produced, though this was not revealed until much later. South Africa thereby became the *only* country

---

* Robert Frasure was killed in an accident near Sarajevo during the negotiations which led to the Dayton Peace accord and cease-fire in Bosnia.

ever to develop a nuclear weapons capability and then renounce it.

The central issue, however, was what was to be done about Mandela and the ANC. De Klerk took the view that he had to create the right climate before he could consider releasing Mandela. The tolerance of peaceful demonstrations and effective ending of attempts to censor the press were important steps in that direction.

Some time before, the South African government had released one senior ANC leader, Govan Mbeki. There were several others still imprisoned with Mandela, including Walter Sisulu. We argued hard, for many weeks, for the release of Sisulu and the other long-term prisoners as the next step. On 15 October 1989, Sisulu and all Mandela's other senior ANC colleagues were released.

It was an emotional homecoming as they invited us to meet them in Soweto. None of these venerable old gentlemen wearing cardigans or waistcoats looked much like revolutionaries, though several were members of the South African Communist Party. I was pleased, especially, for Albertina Sisulu, a stalwart of the ANC's women's movement, who was universally admired in Soweto, unlike some of her counterparts.

We were now on the verge of another Commonwealth Conference in Kuala Lumpur and I had used its proximity, unashamedly, as a way to try to accelerate the release of Walter Sisulu and his companions. Margaret Thatcher enjoyed yet another fracas about South Africa with her fellow heads of government rather more than her new Foreign Secretary, John Major, whose efforts to work out an agreed communiqué she disavowed. Inadequate recognition, she felt, was being given to the changes being brought about by De Klerk. It was the least appropriate time to be considering further sanctions. Given that Mandela's release followed within four months of this meeting, she considered that she was justified.

We were now entering the critical phase. There was no doubt in my mind that De Klerk wanted to release Mandela, but he was going to need some help and encouragement. I returned to London to see Douglas Hurd, who had just taken over as Foreign Secretary. I explained that in our continuing exchanges with De Klerk, in which we were urging him to release Mandela and un-ban the ANC, he was going to want to know what *we* would do if he did take those steps. The obvious response would be to rescind the ban on new investment. That would enable De Klerk to demonstrate that this fundamental step had produced a response, at any rate from us. Douglas Hurd was strongly in favour of doing this. I pointed out that there would be a storm of criticism from those, including the rest of the Commonwealth, who wanted nothing done until the attainment of one man, one vote. Nor would anyone else follow us immediately, though I was sure some would do so in due course. Douglas Hurd was unfazed by the idea of doing this on our own – a position strongly endorsed by Margaret Thatcher.

So, on my return to South Africa, I was able to tell De Klerk that if he took these steps, there would be a response from us. De Klerk relayed this to the members of his Cabinet in their meeting on the eve of the opening of Parliament.

De Klerk spent the evening working on his speech. At around midnight, he telephoned me to say that I could tell my Prime Minister that she would not be disappointed. He added that the US television were reporting that he was about to release Mandela. This was not the case as practical steps had to be taken to prepare for his release and Mandela himself was insisting on this. I told De Klerk that he would get the fullest possible support from us.

And so we gathered on the morning of 2 February 1990, in our morning-suits, the ladies all in hats, for the opening of Parliament. Andries Treurnicht and his cohorts walked out as De Klerk announced the un-banning of the ANC and the South African Communist Party, the freeing of political prisoners, the suspension of capital punishment and the lifting of many of the restrictions imposed under the state of emergency. Eight days later De Klerk gave me a few hours' notice of his intention to announce the release of Nelson Mandela.

Mandela was released at 3 p.m. on 11 February. The celebration of his release nearly turned into a disaster. At the first attempt, it proved impossible for his car to get through the enormous crowd to Cape Town's City Hall. As the crowd grew restive, a second and this time successful attempt was made and Mandela addressed the world's television audience as well as his compatriots in the square below. In his early statements Mandela stressed his continuing commitment to the armed struggle, as well as to negotiations.

17 Mandela

Five days after his release from jail, I met Mandela in Johannesburg. Greeting me very warmly, he asked for his best wishes to be passed to Mrs Thatcher – rather to the amazement of the attendant press, who considered her to be the *bête noire* of the ANC.

The ANC in fact were very worried, and rightly so, about Mandela's security and did not want this to be entrusted mainly to the South African police. We offered to do what we could to help over this and ended up training his personal bodyguards.

I arranged to call on Mandela in the modest four-roomed house he had returned to in Soweto. He declined at first to move into the large house his wife had built – nicknamed by the Sowetans 'Beverly Hills'. The contrast was dramatic between these humble surroundings and the quality of the man inside. His old-world courtesy and unfailing charm served at times to mask a steely determination not to compromise any of the principles for which he and others had sacrificed their liberty or lives. He was, he emphasized, the servant of his party, the African National Congress, and not its master. It was, he insisted to me, not a party, but a movement intended to embody the aspirations of all South Africans. He had difficulty accepting that the ANC could be wrong, and even in understanding that others might not wish to join it. Yet he showed a much greater commitment than others to genuine political tolerance and acceptance that South Africa must be a society with which all sections of the population could identify, including his former oppressors.

Mandela was well aware of the part we, along of course with many others, had played in pressing for his release and that we did have more influence than most others on the South African government. I explained the issues on which he would find us firm allies – the release of prisoners, the return of the exiled leaders and other ANC members from Lusaka, the attainment of genuine majority rule. I also explained that we did not believe in disinvestment – a subject which was never mentioned by Mandela in his speeches – and urged him not to continue calling for the nationalization of the banks and mines. I encouraged him to arrange a meeting with Buthelezi, which he seemed disposed to do. As in all my meetings with Mandela, I got an extremely friendly and sympathetic hearing.

But when Mandela attended the Namibia independence celebrations, he declined to meet Douglas Hurd, fuelling press stories of a 'snub', and avoided a meeting with the Prime Minister when, in April, he flew in and out of Britain to attend a concert at Wembley to raise money for the ANC. The external wing of the ANC continued to hold against Mrs Thatcher her opposition to further sanctions. Mandela, however, had a different attitude. He told me he appreciated the role she had played in pressing for his release and that he wanted to meet her – but at a time when the rest of the movement had been reconciled to the idea.

Given the flood of visitors and meetings over which he had to preside, Mandela could no longer continue to live in the tiny house in Soweto which had been his former home. He was resigned to moving into his wife's house in Diepkloof, but here too there were security problems. We provided a small amount of money to build a wall high enough to prevent passers-by peering into the dining-room.

With the ANC still in a state of extreme disorganization, there followed an inadvertently hilarious episode as I arranged to meet Mandela one afternoon, as scheduled, at his party headquarters in Johannesburg. I arrived there to be told that Nelson Mandela was busy meeting me at the British Embassy in Pretoria – where the rest of the staff were delighted to encounter the great man.

As Mandela told me, his inclination was to have an early meeting with Buthelezi. The ANC and Inkatha for the past five years had been in a state of undeclared war. But Buthelezi had refused to negotiate with the South African government so long as Mandela remained in jail. Whatever their political differences, they needed jointly to take action to curb the violence between their supporters. Addressing a meeting in Durban in February, Mandela urged the ANC crowd to throw their weapons into the sea. This, unfortunately, had no effect. The fighting between Inkatha and the ANC continued unabated. When Mandela announced to ANC supporters at a meeting in the Natal Midlands that he intended to meet Buthelezi, he was disconcerted to find the crowd turning against him and decided not to pursue the idea. This area was the fiefdom of the hard-line Communist, indeed Stalinist, ANC leader, Harry Gwala. While Inkatha had its warlords, so did the ANC, and Gwala was the most prominent of them. A few months earlier, I had argued with the government for his release. In no other instance did I think I had been mistaken in doing so; but I must confess to having had second thoughts in the case of Harry Gwala. The decision to put off a meeting with Buthelezi was to prove expensive.

Mandela was now planning to visit the United States, to be followed by a visit to London to meet Mrs Thatcher. I visited him in a private hospital in Johannesburg shortly before his departure. He had been admitted suffering from exhaustion. I explained that we were extremely worried about his schedule in the United States, where he was expected to visit seven cities in ten days. To give him some rest before doing so, we were arranging for him and Oliver Tambo (the ANC President) to spend a quiet weekend together in the English countryside, on his way to America.

When he met Mrs Thatcher, I said, he would find her genuinely determined to get rid of apartheid and not the least effective of its opponents. We would support Mandela's demands for a constitution based on genuine majority rule, with normal protections for minority rights. I warned that the Prime Minister would not agree to give funds to the ANC, as the Australian and Scandinavian governments were doing. Instead we were further expanding what was already by far the largest programme of projects in the townships, support for low-cost housing and scholarships for black South Africans.

I congratulated Mandela on not having used the word 'nationalization' once in the previous months! 'But it was your idea', Mandela replied, referring to the influence of the London School of Economics and others on budding African politicians in the 1950s. 'It was fashionable then', he added with a smile. I replied that it certainly was not fashionable now. Mandela thanked me warmly for these 'tips' for his meeting with the Prime Minister. Mandela telephoned Mrs Thatcher before departing for the United States to thank us for arranging the weekend with Tambo, only to receive a stern lecture about his schedule.

Mandela arrived in London, as I had feared, with a chest infection and utterly exhausted by his tour of America. I saw Mrs Thatcher before the meeting. Mandela, I told her, was no Communist and it was the regime that had forced him to threaten violence. His own activities in that regard had been limited to trying to blow up a few electricity pylons. He was as remarkable a human being as I had ever met – and one of nature's great gentlemen. He had waited 27 years for the chance to tell her and other heads of government his story.

The meeting lasted three hours, with the Prime Minister very concerned about Mandela's state of health. As he put it, 'she chided me like a school-marm for not taking her advice and cutting down on my schedule'.* She listened, asking no more than a couple of questions, as he explained to her for an hour the history of the ANC and the difficulties he was facing in negotiations. He thanked her for the pressure she had exerted for his release and for the support he was receiving from us, but made no head-way with a plea for more sanctions. Over lunch, there was an intense discussion of economic policy and the sort of constitution which ought to emerge and which we could support. The meeting lasted so long that members of the press waiting outside began to chant: 'Free Nelson Mandela!' Mandela felt that it had gone well and, rather to the dismay of some of her domestic opponents, emerged on the doorstep of 10 Downing Street to pay tribute to the Prime Minister for the role she had played in helping to secure his release.

In South Africa, relations remained very tense between the ANC leaders and the government. The country was suffering from a fresh upsurge in violence, especially in Natal and the townships around Johannesburg, where clashes

---

* Nelson Mandela, *Long Walk to Freedom* (Boston: Little, Brown, 1994), p. 509.

between ANC and Inkatha supporters were a daily occurrence. The ANC had not yet formally suspended the armed struggle. We and others were urging them to do so, believing that we could then get more normalizing moves from the government. This important step was taken in August. Among those who had argued for it to be taken was Joe Slovo. Notwithstanding his avuncular manner and apparently revisionist beliefs, Joe Slovo had defended every twist and turn of Stalin and his successors, quarrelling in the process with his more independently minded wife and fellow-Communist, Ruth First, killed in Maputo by a parcel bomb despatched by South African military intelligence. By the time he returned to South Africa, however, the Vatican in which he believed had collapsed and I was not alone in finding that Joe Slovo, with Thabo Mbeki, acted at times as a moderating influence on Mandela, who was prone to react more emotionally each time some new act of violence occurred or negotiations reached apparent deadlock.

Mandela was convinced, with good reason, that sections of the police and others were encouraging Inkatha attacks on ANC supporters. But this was not the root cause of the violence, for which the responsibility was shared by both sides, and I continued to argue for a meeting with Buthelezi, whom I also was seeing regularly in Ulundi. De Klerk felt that the ANC were not doing enough to restrain violence by their own supporters.

By this stage I was receiving a good deal of hate-mail from right-wing Afrikaners suggesting, implausibly, that I was Lord Milner reincarnated and bent on the destruction of the Boers. Some of this came from a faction led by Piet 'Skiet' Rudolph, which had carried out a number of armed attacks. One Sunday morning shots were fired at the Embassy in Pretoria. The intent appeared to be not to inflict any serious damage, but to issue some kind of warning.

Mandela, meanwhile, continued to tour abroad, intensifying his efforts to raise funds for the ANC. I was conscious of the fact that, among his overseas visitors, I was the one who tended to take him less agreeable news. A good many others came rather to worship at the shrine. It was a remarkable commentary on the quality of this extraordinary man that, far from resenting such expressions of difference of view, he seemed positively to welcome them and find them more interesting than unadulterated adulation.

When he returned from a visit to Libya, I saw him to suggest that it surely was a mistake to have described Qadhafi, publicly, as 'a great supporter of human rights'! But Mandela was determined to stand by those who had helped the ANC in their struggle, and were continuing to provide financial support.

On another occasion, discussing Inkatha, Mandela suggested that they had only the support of 1 per cent of the population. When I queried this, he brandished a copy of *The Economist*, which indeed suggested that this was so – on the basis of a survey of the townships in the Transvaal. I replied that in rural, feudal Zululand north of the Tugela, Mandela would find that Inkatha had 100 per cent support. As the ANC contended that Inkatha alone were responsible for the violence, I handed him the photograph of a group of young 'comrades' necklacing a Zulu hostel dweller. While he had difficulty believing that these really were ANC supporters – despite the logos on their chests – Mandela began to make more and firmer statements calling on both sides to end the violence.

After numerous meetings with Mandela in Soweto, I suggested that, next time, we should lunch together at the best restaurant in Johannesburg. It is hard to imagine today the commotion this caused at the time – the intake of breath as we revealed, at the last minute, the identity of our guest and the reactions of the other diners, most of whom had voted to keep him for three decades in jail, as he shook hands with every one, as if they were his natural supporters. It was a bravura performance, often to be repeated, and calculated very deliberately to win over the most irreconcilable of his opponents – just as he had succeeded in co-opting his warders in jail.

At this stage the Foreign Affairs Committee of the House of Commons descended on us in Pretoria. A party I gave for them was the first occasion on which we, or anyone else for that matter, had been able to gather under the same roof members of the government, ANC leaders including the Delmas treason triallists, members of the PAC and AZAPO and the redoubtable Koos van der Merwe, representing the extreme right-wing Conservative Party. Khulu Sibiya enquired publicly in *City Press* the next day why it was that such a gathering could only be held in a foreign embassy and, before too long, what hitherto had seemed unthinkable started to become the norm.

In December the ANC held its first large conference in South Africa in three decades. Oliver and Adelaide Tambo returned for the conference. Oliver Tambo, though still formally President of the ANC, by now was very frail. He had received me with great kindness in his house in Highgate at a time when the British government still were supposed not to be talking to the ANC. A most unlikely revolutionary, he had invited me to dinner with Mandela with a card bearing the words 'carriages at eleven o'clock'! When an over-eager colleague tried to see the Tambos on the day of their return, he was sent away with the message that they wanted to see 'our Ambassador'. On the following day, I was summoned to see them in Soweto, where I was entertained by Adelaide with tea and currant cakes. It was moving to see Oliver Tambo back in his country at last and a tragedy that he was by then so close to the end of his life.

At the conference, Oliver Tambo invited the ANC to reconsider its policy on sanctions. Other governments, he pointed out, were unlikely to want to maintain sanctions against De Klerk. This got a frosty reception from the party militants who continued to insist – as did their external supporters – that 'nothing had changed'.

Nelson Mandela by now was badly in need of a rest. He confided to me that he had been offered a three weeks' holiday and medical treatment in Cuba. We urged him not to accept, pointing out how much support he would forfeit in the United States if he did. I suggested Kangwane, having stayed there myself. It was a suggestion rapidly adopted by Mandela, who loved the bush, and he stayed with his friend Enos Mabuza, and telephoned to give me the politically incorrect news that he had succeeded in shooting a buck.

Oliver Tambo, I discovered, favoured a meeting between Mandela and Buthelezi to try to arrest the violence and in January 1991 this took place at the Royal Hotel in Durban. It was nine months overdue. Mandela made a very conciliatory statement and thanked Buthelezi for pressing for his release. Buthelezi complained bitterly about his treatment at the hands of the ANC. There was no follow-up to the meeting. No joint committee was established to help combat the violence, which quickly resumed again.

Mandela was more than ever convinced that elements of the security forces were responsible for arming Inkatha – who pointed out that the ANC had their own arms caches – and black groups responsible for horrendous attacks on the commuter trains to and from Soweto. In April, he suspended negotiations, demanding the dismissal of General Malan and the Minister of Law and Order, the phasing out of the hostels in which the mine-workers – many of them Inkatha supporters – lived in the townships and a ban on carrying of 'traditional' weapons by the Zulus.

As the deadline for this ultimatum expired, the press held their breath. Mandela, meanwhile, was spending the evening enjoying the efforts of the greatest jazz musicians in Soweto at the house of his and our friend Clive Menell, who had helped many ANC members in their times of great difficulty. Having talked to Mandela and De Klerk, I was convinced that notwithstanding horrific incidents of violence, the negotiations on which the future of the country depended would be resumed.

In one of my last meetings with Mandela before leaving South Africa, I mentioned to him the need to help De Klerk demonstrate to his supporters that there were some rewards for the changes he was imposing on them. What I had in mind was the lifting of the sports boycott, which I had always regarded as one of the most effective sanctions, as it really did bring home to white South Africans – on a subject about which they felt passionately – the full extent of their isolation. For the ANC, Steve Tshwete had by this time succeeded in forcing the integration of the governing bodies of several major sports. Mandela, after much debate within his party, decided to agree to a provisional lifting of the sports boycott. I have not the slightest doubt that the readmission of South Africa to international sport had a powerful impact on the subsequent referendum of the white population, in which De Klerk sought and secured their support for the course on which he had embarked.

Mandela, meanwhile, was very much affected by the trial

of his wife, which had begun in February. Winnie Mandela was accused following the kidnapping of four youths and murder of one of them by members of her 'football team' at her home in Soweto. Mandela, at the time still convinced of her innocence, told me that he blamed himself for her difficulties, having been unable to offer her any effective support throughout his years in prison.

Six months before, Margaret Thatcher had been deposed as Prime Minister by her fellow members of the Conservative Party and replaced by John Major. De Klerk regarded it as a debt of honour to invite her to visit South Africa. The visit was bound to be tricky in some respects, as the more militant members of the ANC were threatening to stage demonstrations against her. Since we were by now familiar with their tactics, it was easy enough to thwart them by the simple expedient of not announcing in advance the details of her programme.

In Cape Town De Klerk gave a state dinner in her honour. During a visit to the Independent Development Trust, which we supported, the police were alarmed when a crowd gathered outside – only to burst into applause when she emerged. More predictably, she got a similar reception from the students in the Afrikaner citadel of Stellenbosch.

Cyril Ramaphosa, head of the National Union of Mineworkers and a senior figure in the ANC, had expressed to me one major worry about her visit. This was that the city council had declared their intention of awarding her the freedom of the city of Johannesburg. Ramaphosa warned me that if this happened, there were bound to be demonstrations. I assured him that she had no intention of receiving this award from an all-white council which represented a tiny fraction of the people of Johannesburg. Instead we took her to Soweto, where she got a warm reception at the Bharagwanath hospital and from Aggrey Klaaste at the *Sowetan*.

Having spent two days with De Klerk and his wife at the Mala Mala game reserve, I accompanied Mrs Thatcher on the last leg of her visit, to meet Buthelezi at Ulundi. She was greeted by the usual array of Zulu warriors with their *assegais* and shields and visited the battlefield on which the British army finally had managed to defeat the Zulus.

Mandela told me that he was keen to meet her, having just stated publicly that the ANC 'had much to thank her for', despite their disagreements about sanctions. But he was confronted by a deputation from the youth wing protesting against such a meeting. He therefore proposed that they should talk at length on the telephone, which they did while she was at Mala Mala. Though she was no friend of the liberation movements, it was thanks to her willingness to take the necessary risks that we had been able to end the Rhodesian war. Through four years in South Africa, I had received no instructions but full backing from her.

I was now on the verge of leaving South Africa to take up my post as Ambassador in Washington. I travelled from Ulundi to Pretoria for a farewell party given by my deputy, Anthony Rowell. I arrived to find Mandela there, together with his wife, who swept me off my feet in a bear-like embrace. They were accompanied by Thabo Mbeki, Jacob Zuma and much of the rest of the ANC hierarchy. Mandela had made a special effort to make the long journey from Soweto, as at the time he still hated visiting Pretoria, where most of his previous experiences had been at police headquarters. Among our friends there was Johan Heyns.

Having talked over my last few days in South Africa to all the main political leaders, I left convinced that the process was indeed irreversible and that agreement would be reached on a fully democratic constitution. There would be a lot more violence and turbulence, some serious set-backs and apparent breakdowns. But Mandela and De Klerk knew that in the end they were condemned to agree. I did not believe that De Klerk, having gone this far, would try to stop halfway. I felt sure that in due course we would see an ANC government, led by Mandela, with De Klerk and the National Party participating in it. My main worry was whether an accommodation could also be reached with Inkatha.

When I left, Wits University, egged on by Helen Suzman, was kind enough to award me an honorary degree 'for services to the struggle against apartheid'. The offer from the South African government of the Order of Good Hope I had to decline – on the same grounds Margaret Thatcher had declined the Freedom of the City of Johannesburg. The ANC leaders and Buthelezi added their good wishes.

It was this that pleased me the most, for it demonstrated that in that deeply divided society, it was possible to try to act as a genuinely honest broker and to retain the confidence of the main participants. That in itself was a demonstration that in the end, they wanted to try to find a way to agree.

I left with an unaccustomed sense of humility. My predecessors, however hard they tried – and some tried harder than others – could not hope to achieve much in the face of that iron-clad regime. And what in the end was achieved was accomplished by and for South Africans – not by any outsider, however well-disposed. The most that any Embassy could do was to try to help act as a facilitator – and then let South Africans get on with a process in which too much foreign involvement was positively undesirable.

For a time the South African government, trying to change but still hard put to bring itself to do so, did feel that it needed one Western country it felt it could appeal to. For a time, Mandela and the ANC also felt they needed someone they could appeal to with, they hoped, some influence on the other side. Within months, there would be little further need, and certainly much less scope, for such a role.

Two and a half years later I was able to fulfil a promise to Mandela that, as soon as he was ready to call for new investment, we would be the first to help him to attract back to South Africa some of the companies which had left and to encourage others to invest. This we did at a dinner and reception he addressed at the British Embassy in Washington, to which we invited a host of American industrialists and investment fund managers. Throwing away his prepared speech, Mandela declared his intention to seek an accommodation with Buthelezi and to re-appoint De Klerk's Finance Minister, Derek Keys.

Several of the South African businessmen travelling in his

wake had been pillars of the apartheid regime. Congratulated on his apparent ability to forget this, Mandela replied with understandable bitterness that he forgot nothing, and nor did he forgive, but that he needed them now. And indeed he did, for the return of foreign investment already was proving much harder to achieve than had been anticipated.

A few weeks later, the first fully democratic elections ever to be held in South Africa resulted in a resounding victory for the ANC, but also in a coalition government in which, despite the tensions between them, all the main political forces for the time being were represented in a still deeply divided society.

Epilogue: After the Honeymoon

The euphoria which marked much of the Western press reporting of these events – particularly in the United States – from the outset alarmed me. First, it was suggested that what happened in South Africa was a 'miracle', which it was not. The fact that ultimate disaster was avoided and a relatively peaceful transition achieved was the work of a vast number of dedicated South Africans, black and white, bent on ensuring that the catastrophe so many outsiders were predicting was avoided.

I also had memories of the post-independence euphoria, when new governments were installed, representing the majority, elsewhere in Africa. They started with high hopes and good intentions – yet, within a few years, many had turned into oppressors themselves. The worst mistake, in every case, was intolerance not of the whites, but of black opponents of the new regime.

This is not a new phenomenon. Thirty years ago my professor at the University of Dakar in Senegal, René Dumont, wrote a prophetic book entitled *L'Afrique noire est mal partie*. In it he described the same phenomenon as in Eastern Europe in the Communist era – the emergence of a new ruling class, the *nomenklatura* or *Wa-benzi*, arrogating to themselves the privileges of their predecessors and creating an unbridgeable gulf between them and the rest of the population.

Throughout most of my time in South Africa, I was convinced that getting rid of apartheid was not going to prove the most intractable problem facing the country. The fundamental difficulty was the near-impossibility of raising living standards for ordinary people when the population is increasing by one million people a year – from 33 million ten years ago to 43 million today.

The post-independence history of most of the rest of Africa has been grim indeed. In few countries are the population better off today than they were at the end of the colonial

156

era. In societies where the only way of changing the government has been by coups and civil wars, it is hardly surprising that the history of post-independence Africa has been
one of coups and civil wars.

While there still are attempts to continue to blame many
of Africa's current ills on the colonial past, the unpleasant
fact is that most of the damage has been self-inflicted. The
constitutions negotiated at the time of independence contained provisions seeking to protect human rights, freedom
of the press, the rule of law and political opposition, most
of which have been honoured in the breach rather than
the observance. Regimes which, initially, were popular have
sought to perpetuate themselves in power irrespective of the
degree of public support. Western governments and aid
agencies have been far too complaisant about the suppression
of democracy and gross violations of human rights, exhibit-
ing an attitude so patronizing as to constitute a singularly
unpleasant form of neo-colonialism – the unstated assumption being that special allowance must be made for African
regimes which cannot be expected to perform, economically
or politically, up to the standards anticipated elsewhere.

In Zimbabwe, a bitter war was followed by a remarkable
example of racial reconciliation. But it also was followed by
the repression in Matabeleland, chronicled by Peter Godwin.*
Great advances have been made with the provision of education and health care. Yet, partly as a result of the population increase, real incomes for most Zimbabweans have not
increased over the past 15 years. The ruling party won the
1996 elections with 29 per cent of the electorate voting and
no opposition candidates standing.

In South Africa's case, the honeymoon lasted just two years,
ending with the withdrawal of the National Party from government, a collapse of the rand and failure to deal with the
wave of violent crime that has engulfed Johannesburg.

While there is every reason to celebrate the extraordinary
achievement and statesmanship of Mandela and De Klerk
in engineering a relatively peaceful transfer of power, the
country now has to prove that it can answer an entirely different and still more difficult question. Can South Africa under,

---

* Peter Godwin, *Mukiwa* (London: Picador, 1996), pp. 329–85.

at last, a property elected and representative government, avoid the fate that has overtaken much of the rest of Africa? It certainly has the potential to do so. For South Africa has a unique combination of skills and resources, a dynamic entrepreneurial class and the largest concentration of industry south of Milan and Barcelona. No less important, and largely as a result of the struggle against apartheid, the democratic forces in South Africa are both stronger and deeper than has proved to be the case elsewhere. What is pretty clear is that South Africa can hope to succeed on the basis of real political and economic freedom and is unlikely to do so otherwise. If it can avoid the guided democracy and silencing of dissent so prevalent elsewhere in the continent, the government will remain responsive to the needs of the population. Wealth must be redistributed, but that can only be achieved through economic growth and not as a zero-sum game.

A start has scarcely yet been made in tackling the immense economic and social problems the new government has inherited – the legacy of apartheid. It surely is deserving of international support in its efforts to overcome them. South Africa, at long last, is a fully democratic society. The future will depend on it remaining so. Therein, and in the degree of economic success that can be achieved, will lie the ultimate test of the proposition that South Africa *can* escape the fate of much of the rest of Africa and, more than that, can help to lead the renaissance of southern Africa I and others would so dearly like to see.

Index